New Zealand Travel Guide

*From Maori Traditions to Thrilling Outdoor
Escapes, Experience the Best of Kiwi Hospitality
and Scenic Wonders*

Noah Bowman

TABLE OF CONTENTS

CHAPTER 1: INTRODUCTION TO NEW ZEALAND

1. New Zealand at a Glance

Nestled in the southwestern Pacific Ocean, New Zealand, a dynamic nation composed of two main islands—the North Island and the South Island—along with numerous smaller isles, captivates with its diverse landscapes and vibrant culture. This land of the long white cloud, or Aotearoa as it is known in Maori, boasts a unique blend of natural beauty and cultural richness, attracting travelers from all corners of the globe.

First-time visitors are often struck by New Zealand's astounding geographical diversity. The North Island is characterized by lush, rolling hills, geothermal wonders, and sprawling urban centers. Auckland, the country's largest city, is a bustling metropolis surrounded by harbors and dotted with volcanic cones. Further south, the geothermal city of Rotorua entices with its bubbling mud pools and spouting geysers, while Wellington, the capital, is renowned for its vibrant arts scene and picturesque harbor. The North Island is also home to stunning beaches, dense native forests, and the majestic peaks of the Central Plateau.

In contrast, the South Island presents a different palette of natural wonders. This island is a paradise for adventure seekers and nature lovers alike. The Southern Alps, a breathtaking mountain range stretching along the island's spine, offers unrivaled opportunities for skiing, hiking, and mountaineering. Fiordland National Park, a UNESCO World Heritage Site, is a place of dramatic cliffs and serene waters, where the ethereal beauty of Milford Sound captivates all who visit. The South Island is also known for its expansive vineyards, particularly in the Marlborough region, where world-class wines are crafted.

New Zealand's climate is as varied as its landscapes. The country enjoys a temperate maritime climate, with mild temperatures and moderate rainfall throughout the year. The North Island tends to be warmer, with sub-tropical summers in the far north, while the South Island experiences cooler temperatures, especially in the alpine regions. This diversity in climate allows for a wide range of activities year-round, from sun-soaked beach escapades to snowy alpine adventures.

Beyond its physical allure, New Zealand is a nation with a rich tapestry of history and culture. The Maori, the indigenous Polynesian people of New Zealand, have a profound influence on the country's identity. Their traditions, language, and art are woven into the fabric of everyday life, offering a unique cultural experience. Visitors can engage with Maori culture through performances of traditional song and dance, known as kapa haka, or by visiting marae—sacred meeting grounds where the community gathers for ceremonies and celebrations.

The European settlers, who arrived later, brought with them their own customs, blending with the existing Maori culture to create a distinctive Kiwi identity. This fusion is evident in New Zealand's vibrant art scene, eclectic cuisine, and lively festivals, which celebrate everything from music and dance to food and wine.

For those seeking adventure, New Zealand is a veritable playground. Its varied landscapes allow for a multitude of outdoor pursuits. The country is renowned for its hiking trails, known locally as "tramping," which traverse some of the most breathtaking terrains imaginable. The Great Walks, a network of premier tracks, offer the chance to explore pristine wilderness areas, from the coastal beauty of the Abel Tasman Track to the alpine vistas of the Routeburn Track.

Water sports enthusiasts will find no shortage of activities, with opportunities for kayaking, sailing, and surfing along New Zealand's extensive coastline. The country's rivers and lakes are perfect for fishing and white-water rafting, while the clear blue waters of the Bay of Islands provide an idyllic setting for diving and snorkeling.

New Zealand is also a haven for wildlife enthusiasts. The country's isolation has resulted in a unique array of flora and fauna, including the iconic kiwi bird, a national symbol. Visitors can encounter a range of native species in the many national parks and reserves scattered across the islands. Whale watching off the coast of Kaikoura, and encounters with playful dolphins and sea lions, offer unforgettable experiences.

Despite its remote location, New Zealand is easily accessible. The country has a well-connected network of domestic flights, making it convenient to travel between the North and South Islands. Additionally, a robust system of buses and trains provides affordable and scenic travel options. For those who prefer to explore at their own pace, renting a car or campervan is a popular choice, offering the freedom to discover hidden gems off the beaten path.

Kiwi hospitality is legendary, and visitors can expect a warm welcome wherever they go. New Zealanders, or "Kiwis," are known for their friendly and laid-back nature, making it easy for travelers to feel at home. The country's accommodation options are diverse, ranging from luxury lodges and boutique hotels to budget-friendly hostels and holiday parks.

In recent years, New Zealand has become increasingly conscious of sustainability and eco-tourism. Efforts to preserve the natural environment and protect native species are evident in the many conservation programs and eco-friendly initiatives across the country. Travelers are encouraged to respect the land and embrace the principles of kaitiakitanga, a Maori concept of guardianship and conservation.

With its stunning landscapes, rich cultural heritage, and endless opportunities for adventure, New Zealand offers a travel experience like no other. Whether you're seeking thrills in the great outdoors, immersing yourself in Maori culture, or simply relaxing amidst breathtaking scenery, this remarkable country promises a journey of discovery and wonder.

2. Historical Overview

New Zealand's history weaves a rich tapestry of exploration, settlement, and cultural fusion, beginning long before European arrival. The first chapter of this story belongs to the Maori, Polynesian navigators who embarked on epic voyages across the Pacific Ocean. Guided by the stars and ocean currents, they settled in Aotearoa around the 13th century, bringing with them a vibrant culture that has shaped the nation's identity.

The Maori society was organized into iwi (tribes) and hapū (sub-tribes), each with their own distinct traditions and territories. They were skilled horticulturalists, cultivating crops like kumara (sweet potato) and taro. Their society was also marked by intricate carvings, tattoos, and oral traditions, with myths and legends passed down through generations. The Maori worldview, deeply rooted in the natural environment, emphasized the interconnectedness of all living things and the spiritual significance of the land.

European contact began in the 17th century with Dutch explorer Abel Tasman, who sighted the western coasts of New Zealand in 1642. This initial encounter was brief and marred by violence, as misunderstandings led to a clash with the Maori. It wasn't until over a century later, in 1769, that British explorer Captain James Cook made landfall. Cook's expeditions mapped the coastline and established more enduring relationships with the Maori, laying the groundwork for future interactions.

The early 19th century saw an influx of European settlers and whalers, drawn by New Zealand's abundant resources. This period marked the beginning of significant change for the Maori, as they engaged in trade and adopted new technologies, but also faced challenges such as disease and land disputes. The introduction of Christianity by missionaries further influenced Maori society, leading to shifts in cultural practices and beliefs.

The signing of the Treaty of Waitangi in 1840 was a pivotal moment in New Zealand's history. This treaty, signed between the British Crown and various Maori chiefs, aimed to establish British sovereignty while guaranteeing Maori rights to their lands and resources. However, differing interpretations of the treaty's terms soon led to conflict. The Maori understood it as a partnership, while the British saw it as a means to assert control. These discrepancies fueled tensions, culminating in a series of conflicts known as the New Zealand Wars, which lasted from the 1840s to the 1870s.

The wars had significant repercussions, with many Maori losing land and autonomy. Despite this, Maori culture persisted, adapting and evolving in the face of adversity. The late 19th and early 20th centuries saw continued land loss through sales and confiscations, but also a resurgence of Maori identity and activism. Efforts to preserve language and traditions gained momentum, laying the foundation for future cultural revitalization.

By the mid-20th century, New Zealand was undergoing transformation as an increasingly multicultural society. The postwar period brought economic growth and urbanization, drawing Maori from rural areas to cities in search of employment and opportunities. This migration led to the emergence of a dynamic urban Maori culture, blending traditional practices with contemporary influences.

Simultaneously, the country was forging its national identity on the global stage. Participation in international conflicts, such as the World Wars, solidified New Zealand's reputation as a staunch ally. The nation's unique position as a Pacific nation with strong ties to both Europe and the indigenous Maori continued to shape its diplomatic and cultural outlook.

The latter half of the 20th century witnessed significant social and political change. The Maori protest movement gained momentum, advocating for land rights, language preservation, and recognition of treaty obligations. These efforts culminated in the establishment of the Waitangi Tribunal in 1975, tasked with addressing historical grievances and facilitating reconciliation between Maori and the Crown.

Today, New Zealand stands as a testament to the resilience and adaptability of its people. The Maori Renaissance, a cultural and political resurgence that began in the late 20th century, has revitalized Maori language, arts, and traditions. Maori culture is celebrated and integrated into the broader national identity, influencing everything from education and business to sports and entertainment.

Concurrently, New Zealand's commitment to multiculturalism is evident in its diverse population, which includes people of European, Maori, Pacific Islander, and Asian descent. This diversity enriches the nation's cultural landscape, fostering a spirit of openness and inclusivity.

As New Zealand navigates the challenges of the 21st century, its history serves as a reminder of the importance of understanding and respecting the past. The lessons learned from the Treaty of Waitangi, the struggles for justice and equality, and the celebration of cultural diversity all contribute to a society that values unity and progress.

In reflecting on New Zealand's historical journey, one can appreciate the intricate interplay between tradition and modernity, and the enduring legacy of those who have shaped this remarkable nation. As the story of New Zealand continues to unfold, it remains a land of promise and potential, where the threads of history are woven into the fabric of the present, guiding the path to the future.

3. Understanding the Maori Culture

The Maori culture, a cornerstone of New Zealand's identity, offers a rich tapestry of traditions, beliefs, and practices that have endured for centuries. To truly appreciate the essence of Aotearoa, one must delve into the vibrant world of the Maori, the indigenous Polynesian people whose ancestors navigated the vast Pacific Ocean to settle in this land.

Central to Maori culture is the concept of whakapapa, or genealogy, which establishes connections between individuals, families, and the natural world. Whakapapa is more than a lineage; it is a framework that binds the Maori to their ancestors and the land, weaving past, present, and future into a single continuum. This perspective fosters a deep sense of belonging and responsibility, as each person is a guardian of their ancestral heritage and the environment.

The Maori worldview is steeped in spirituality, with a belief system that acknowledges the presence of atua, or gods, who govern various aspects of life and nature. These deities are honored through rituals and ceremonies, such as the powhiri, a formal welcome that involves speeches, songs, and the hongi—a traditional greeting where individuals press their noses together to share the breath of life. Through these practices, the Maori express their reverence for the divine and their interconnectedness with the universe.

Art and storytelling are vital components of Maori culture, serving as vehicles for preserving history and knowledge. Whakairo, or carving, is a revered art form that adorns meeting houses, canoes, and personal adornments with intricate designs. Each carving tells a story, capturing the essence of ancestors, legends, and the natural world. Similarly, weaving, known as raranga, transforms flax into decorative and functional items, showcasing the skill and creativity of Maori artisans.

The oral tradition, anchored in the recital of whakapapa, legends, and proverbs, ensures the transmission of cultural wisdom across generations. These narratives, rich with symbolism and metaphor, offer insights into the values and principles that guide Maori life. The legend of Maui, a demi-god known for his cunning and bravery, is one such story that illustrates themes of resilience, ingenuity, and the quest for knowledge.

Language is another cornerstone of Maori culture, with Te Reo Maori being recognized as an official language of New Zealand. Efforts to revitalize and promote the language have been central to the Maori Renaissance, reflecting a broader commitment to cultural preservation. Today, Te Reo is taught in schools, spoken in homes, and used in media, reinforcing its status as a living, dynamic language.

Maori society is organized into iwi and hapū, with each group maintaining its own identity, traditions, and leadership. The marae, a communal meeting place, serves as the heart of Maori social life, where gatherings, ceremonies, and discussions take place. It is here that the principles of manaakitanga, or hospitality, and kotahitanga, or unity, are practiced, strengthening the bonds between individuals and communities.

The traditional Maori diet was shaped by the natural environment, with a reliance on seafood, birds, and native plants. The hangi, a method of cooking food in an earth oven, remains a popular culinary practice, symbolizing the importance of sharing and community in Maori culture. Today, Maori cuisine continues to evolve, incorporating contemporary influences while honoring its roots.

Land is sacred to the Maori, embodying their spiritual and cultural identity. The concept of kaitiakitanga, or guardianship, underscores their duty to protect and preserve the environment for future generations. This relationship with the land is evident in the Maori approach to resource management, which emphasizes sustainability and balance.

Maori culture is dynamic, continually adapting to the challenges and opportunities of the modern world. The Maori Renaissance, a period of cultural revitalization that began in the latter half of the 20th century, has seen a resurgence of interest in language, arts, and identity. This movement has empowered Maori communities, fostering pride and resilience in the face of historical adversity.

Education has played a pivotal role in this cultural revival, with initiatives such as kohanga reo (language nests) and kura kaupapa Maori (Maori immersion schools) providing young people with a strong foundation in their heritage. These programs have been instrumental in nurturing a new generation of Maori leaders who are committed to preserving and promoting their culture.

Maori influence permeates many aspects of New Zealand society, from the arts and literature to sports and politics. The haka, a traditional war dance, has gained international recognition through its association with the All Blacks, New Zealand's national rugby team. This powerful performance embodies the spirit of challenge and unity, captivating audiences around the world.

In the political arena, Maori representation has been enshrined in the New Zealand Parliament for over a century, ensuring that Maori voices are heard in the nation's decision-making processes. The establishment of the Waitangi Tribunal has also been instrumental in addressing historical grievances and fostering dialogue between Maori and the Crown.

Maori culture is not monolithic; it is as diverse as the people who identify with it. Each iwi and hapū contributes to the rich mosaic of Maori identity, bringing unique perspectives and experiences to the broader narrative. This diversity is celebrated through festivals, such as Te Matatini, a biennial kapa haka competition that showcases the best of Maori performing arts.

As the world becomes increasingly interconnected, the Maori continue to navigate the complexities of cultural preservation and adaptation. By maintaining their traditions while embracing innovation, the Maori demonstrate the resilience and vitality of their culture.

In understanding Maori culture, one gains a deeper appreciation for the values and principles that define New Zealand as a nation. The Maori story is an integral part of the country's identity, offering lessons in respect, stewardship, and community that resonate far beyond its shores. Through their enduring legacy, the Maori invite us all to reflect on our own connections to the past, the land, and each other.

4. Geography and Climate

New Zealand, a nation defined by its geographical diversity, spans two main islands—the North and South Islands—along with numerous smaller islets, all of which contribute to its stunning landscapes and unique ecosystems. The country's location in the southwestern Pacific Ocean places it in a prime position for an array of geographical features, from jagged mountain ranges to lush plains and dramatic coastlines. This diverse geography not only shapes the natural beauty of the land but also influences the climate and lifestyle of its inhabitants.

The North Island, known for its volcanic activity and geothermal features, is home to a variety of landscapes. The central region is dominated by the volcanic plateau, where active volcanoes like Mount Ruapehu and Mount Ngauruhoe rise dramatically against the skyline. This area is also home to the Tongariro National Park, a UNESCO World Heritage Site famous for its breathtaking hiking trails and unique volcanic landscapes. The geothermal city of Rotorua, with its bubbling mud pools and steaming geysers, offers a glimpse into the Earth's fiery heart.

In contrast, the North Island's coastal regions boast golden beaches and rugged cliffs. The Coromandel Peninsula, with its pristine beaches and lush native forests, is a popular destination for both relaxation and adventure. The Bay of Islands, a subtropical paradise with over 140 islands, offers opportunities for sailing, diving, and exploring rich marine life. Auckland, the largest city, is built around two harbors and is surrounded by extinct volcanic cones, providing a striking urban landscape.

The South Island presents a different geographical tapestry. The Southern Alps, a majestic mountain range running the length of the island, create a dramatic backbone. Aoraki/Mount Cook, the highest peak in New Zealand, towers over the landscape, offering challenging climbs and awe-inspiring views. The West Coast is characterized by dense rainforests, rugged coastlines, and the unique glaciers of Franz Josef and Fox, which descend from the mountains to near sea level—an occurrence rare in the world.

Further south, Fiordland National Park captivates with its deep fiords, carved by ancient glaciers, and towering cliffs. Milford Sound, arguably the most famous of these fiords, draws visitors with its serene beauty and abundant wildlife. The eastern plains of Canterbury provide a stark contrast, with fertile farmlands stretching as far as the eye can see, supporting a thriving agricultural industry.

New Zealand's offshore islands, such as Stewart Island and the Chatham Islands, add to the country's geographical diversity. Stewart Island, located south of the South Island, is largely unspoiled and covered in native forest, offering a sanctuary for wildlife, including the elusive kiwi bird. The Chatham Islands, isolated in the Pacific, boast unique ecosystems and a rich cultural heritage, shaped by both Maori and European influences.

The country's geographical features are closely linked to its climate, which is predominantly temperate maritime. However, the climate varies significantly across regions due to the diverse landscapes. The North Island generally experiences warmer temperatures, with the northernmost regions enjoying a subtropical climate. Summers are warm and humid, while winters are mild and wet. This climate supports lush vegetation and a vibrant agricultural industry, particularly in regions like Hawke's Bay and the Bay of Plenty, known for their orchards and vineyards.

The South Island, influenced by the Southern Alps, experiences a more diverse climate. The west coast is one of the wettest areas in the country, with heavy rainfall nurturing dense rainforests. In contrast, the eastern regions, sheltered by the mountains, often experience dry, sunny conditions, particularly in areas like Canterbury and Otago. The alpine areas of the Southern Alps receive significant snowfall in winter, creating ideal conditions for skiing and snowboarding.

New Zealand's weather patterns are also influenced by its surrounding ocean, which moderates temperatures and contributes to the country's changeable weather. The prevailing westerly winds, known as the Roaring Forties, bring moisture-laden air across the Tasman Sea, resulting in frequent rain and wind, particularly on the west coast. This maritime influence ensures that no part of the country is too far from the sea, contributing to the coastal character of New Zealand life.

The variability in climate and geography has a profound impact on the flora and fauna of New Zealand. The country's isolation has led to the development of unique ecosystems, home to a diverse range of plant and animal species, many of which are found nowhere else in the world. The native forests, covering large areas of both islands, are dominated by species such as kauri, rimu, and totara, providing habitats for a variety of wildlife.

New Zealand's climate and geography also offer a wealth of outdoor activities and adventures. The country's varied landscapes provide the perfect backdrop for hiking, skiing, surfing, and other recreational pursuits. The Great Walks, a network of premier hiking trails, traverse some of the most spectacular terrains, from coastal paths to alpine tracks, allowing visitors to immerse themselves in the natural beauty of the land.

The diverse climate also supports a thriving agricultural and viticultural industry. New Zealand is renowned for its high-quality produce, including dairy, lamb, and kiwifruit, as well as its world-class wines. The Marlborough region, in particular, is celebrated for its Sauvignon Blanc, benefiting from the sunny, dry climate and fertile soils.

As New Zealand continues to face the challenges of climate change, understanding the intricate relationship between its geography and climate becomes increasingly important. Efforts to conserve the natural environment and protect native species are crucial in preserving the country's unique ecosystems for future generations.

In exploring New Zealand's geography and climate, one gains a deeper appreciation for the natural forces that have shaped this remarkable land. The interplay between mountains, plains, and coastlines creates a dynamic and ever-changing landscape, offering both challenges and opportunities for those who call it home. This geographical diversity not only defines New Zealand's physical character but also influences the cultural and social life of its people, making it a truly unique and captivating destination.

CHAPTER 2: EXPLORING MAORI TRADITIONS

1. The Maori Worldview

The Maori worldview, or "Te Ao Maori," is a profound and integral aspect of New Zealand's cultural landscape, deeply influencing the way of life and philosophy of the Maori people. This perspective is holistic and interconnected, emphasizing the unity of all things and the importance of balance between the spiritual and physical realms. Understanding this worldview offers valuable insights into the values and principles that guide Maori society.

At the heart of the Maori worldview is the concept of whakapapa, or genealogy. Whakapapa is not merely a record of ancestry; it is the foundation of identity and existence. It establishes connections between individuals, families, and the natural world, weaving a web of relationships that extend back to the creation of the universe. Through whakapapa, Maori trace their lineage to the gods, the land, and all living things, reinforcing their role as kaitiaki, or guardians, of the environment.

The Maori cosmos is populated by atua, or gods, each with dominion over specific aspects of life and nature. These deities are integral to the Maori understanding of the world, and their influence is acknowledged in rituals and daily activities. Tangaroa, the god of the sea, is invoked by fishermen, while Tane Mahuta, the god of the forest, is honored by those who gather food and materials from the bush. This relationship with the atua underscores the Maori belief in the sacredness of all things and the need to maintain harmony with the natural world.

Mana, a central concept in Maori culture, refers to spiritual authority and power. It is an intangible force that can be inherited, earned, or bestowed, and it permeates all aspects of life. Individuals, families, and even objects can possess mana, which must be respected and upheld. The loss or diminishment of mana can have serious consequences, affecting one's standing within the community and their relationship with the spiritual realm.

Closely related to mana is tapu, a state of sacredness or restriction. Tapu serves to protect people, places, and objects by designating them as sacred and setting boundaries around their use or interaction. Breaching tapu can result in negative consequences, requiring rituals of purification or restitution to restore balance. This concept reinforces the Maori commitment to preserving the sanctity of life and the natural world.

The principle of utu, or reciprocity, is another key element of the Maori worldview. Utu governs the balance of relationships, ensuring that actions are reciprocated and harmony is maintained within the community. This principle extends to both positive and negative interactions, guiding the resolution of conflicts and the exchange of gifts and services. By adhering to utu, Maori uphold the values of fairness and justice, fostering cohesion and mutual respect.

The Maori worldview is deeply rooted in the land, or whenua, which is considered the source of life and identity. The land is not merely a resource to be exploited; it is a living entity with its own mana and tapu. The bond between the Maori and the land is reflected in the concept of turangawaewae, or "a place to stand." This notion emphasizes the importance of having a connection to one's ancestral land, which provides a sense of belonging and purpose.

Kaitiakitanga, or guardianship, embodies the Maori responsibility to protect and preserve the environment for future generations. This duty is an expression of the interconnectedness of all things and the recognition that the well-being of people is inextricably linked to the health of the land. Kaitiakitanga is practiced through sustainable resource management, conservation efforts, and the revitalization of traditional knowledge.

The Maori worldview also places a strong emphasis on community and collective well-being. Whanaungatanga, or kinship, highlights the importance of relationships and the interconnectedness of individuals within the wider social network. This sense of belonging extends beyond immediate family to include extended kin and the community at large. By prioritizing whanaungatanga, Maori foster a sense of unity and support, ensuring that the needs of all are met.

Education and the transmission of knowledge are vital components of the Maori worldview. Traditional learning is often conducted through oral traditions, storytelling, and practical experience. Elders play a crucial role as custodians of wisdom, passing down cultural knowledge and values to younger generations. This intergenerational exchange ensures the continuity of Maori heritage and reinforces the bonds between past, present, and future.

The Maori worldview is not static; it is dynamic and adaptable, allowing Maori to navigate the complexities of the modern world while remaining true to their cultural roots. This adaptability is evident in the Maori Renaissance, a period of cultural revival that has seen the reassertion of Maori identity and the incorporation of traditional values into contemporary life.

In the realm of politics and governance, the Maori worldview has influenced the development of unique models that integrate traditional leadership structures with modern democratic processes. The establishment of the Maori seats in the New Zealand Parliament and the recognition of Maori customary rights in legislation are examples of how Maori values have been woven into the fabric of national governance.

The Maori worldview offers valuable lessons for addressing contemporary global challenges. Its emphasis on sustainability, community, and interconnectedness provides a framework for fostering harmonious relationships with the environment and each other. By embracing these principles, societies around the world can learn to live in balance with the planet and create a more equitable and resilient future.

In exploring the Maori worldview, one gains a deeper appreciation for the rich cultural heritage that defines New Zealand as a nation. The values of whakapapa, mana, tapu, and kaitiakitanga resonate far beyond the shores of Aotearoa, offering timeless insights into the human experience and our place within the natural world. Through the lens of the Maori worldview, we are reminded of the importance of honoring our connections to each other and the earth, and the enduring legacy of those who have come before us.

2. Traditional Maori Art and Crafts

The realm of traditional Maori art and crafts is a vibrant testament to the creativity, spirituality, and identity of the Maori people. Each piece of art is not merely an object of beauty but a narrative encapsulating the history, beliefs, and values of its creators. This artistic heritage is deeply intertwined with the Maori worldview, reflecting the connection between the spiritual and physical realms, and the relationships between people, their ancestors, and the natural world.

Whakairo, or carving, is one of the most esteemed forms of Maori art, encompassing wood, bone, and stone as mediums. Wood carving, in particular, holds a significant place, as it is used to adorn wharenui (meeting houses), canoes, and weaponry. Each carving is a visual story, often depicting ancestors, deities, and mythological creatures. The intricate patterns and designs are imbued with symbolic meaning, serving as a record of genealogy and tribal history. The art of carving is traditionally passed down through generations, with master carvers, or tohunga whakairo, playing a vital role in preserving this craft.

Bone and stone carvings are also integral to Maori artistry, often crafted into pendants and tools. The hei-tiki, a small carved figure worn around the neck, is one of the most recognized Maori symbols. It is believed to represent an ancestor and is considered a taonga, or treasure, embodying mana and spiritual significance. Greenstone, or pounamu, is highly prized for its beauty and durability and is often used in creating toki (adzes) and mere (clubs), which hold both ceremonial and practical value.

Raranga, or weaving, is another cornerstone of Maori culture, primarily utilizing the leaves of the harakeke, or flax plant. The art of weaving extends beyond the creation of functional items; it is a medium through which stories are told and cultural identity is expressed. The woven patterns, or whatu, often carry symbolic meanings, representing familial ties, spiritual beliefs, and tribal affiliations. Weavers produce a range of items, from everyday objects such as kete (baskets) and whariki (mats) to ceremonial garments like kakahu (cloaks), which are adorned with intricate patterns and sometimes feathers.

The korowai, a type of woven cloak, is a prestigious garment that signifies status and honor. Traditionally worn by chiefs and other esteemed individuals, the korowai is meticulously crafted, with each thread and embellishment chosen for its symbolic significance. The creation of a korowai is a time-intensive process, requiring skill, patience, and a deep understanding of the materials and techniques involved.

The practice of kowhaiwhai, or painted designs, is commonly found on the rafters of wharenui. These painted patterns are characterized by their flowing, symmetrical forms, often representing natural elements such as leaves, waves, and clouds. Kowhaiwhai designs are more than mere decoration; they convey stories and values, linking the community to their ancestors and the natural world. The use of red, black, and white colors is traditional, each holding its own significance and contributing to the visual impact of the designs.

Tukutuku panels, which are lattice-like woven wall decorations, often accompany kowhaiwhai in wharenui. These panels are created using a combination of traditional materials such as toetoe reeds and kiekie vines. The geometric patterns of tukutuku panels are rich in symbolism, with each design conveying specific meanings related to tribal history, genealogy, and mythology. The collaborative nature of creating tukutuku panels, often involving multiple weavers, reflects the communal spirit of Maori society.

Tattooing, or ta moko, is another profound expression of Maori art, serving as a mark of identity, status, and ancestral lineage. Unlike Western tattooing, ta moko is traditionally chiseled into the skin, creating grooves rather than flat images. This practice is deeply personal, with each design unique to the individual and their whakapapa. For men, ta moko often covered the face, buttocks, and thighs, while women typically wore moko kauae on their chins and lips. The revival of ta moko in recent years signifies a reassertion of Maori identity and pride, with contemporary practitioners adapting traditional designs to reflect modern experiences.

The resurgence of traditional Maori art and crafts is part of a broader cultural renaissance that has seen Maori artists and artisans reengage with their heritage while exploring new forms and media. This revitalization is evident in the work of contemporary

Maori artists who draw inspiration from traditional motifs and techniques, infusing them with modern perspectives. The fusion of past and present in Maori art not only preserves cultural traditions but also fosters innovation and dialogue, both within Maori communities and with the wider world.

Educational initiatives and community workshops play a crucial role in sustaining and promoting Maori arts and crafts. By teaching these skills to younger generations, communities ensure that the knowledge and techniques of their ancestors are passed on, keeping the cultural legacy alive. These educational efforts also provide opportunities for cultural exchange and understanding, as people from diverse backgrounds engage with Maori art and its underlying philosophies.

The presence of Maori art in public and private spaces throughout New Zealand is a testament to its enduring significance and the respect it commands. From the intricate carvings that grace marae to the contemporary works displayed in galleries and museums, Maori art continues to captivate and inspire. It serves as a reminder of the richness of Maori culture and the importance of preserving its artistic traditions for future generations.

Through the lens of traditional Maori art and crafts, one gains a deeper appreciation for the values and narratives that define Maori society. These artistic expressions are not static relics of the past; they are living, evolving forms that embody the resilience and creativity of the Maori people. By embracing and celebrating their artistic heritage, the Maori continue to affirm their identity and contribute to the cultural tapestry of New Zealand and beyond.

3. Maori Cuisine and Hangi

Maori cuisine, deeply rooted in the natural bounty of New Zealand, is a reflection of the Maori people's intimate relationship with the land and sea. It is characterized by traditional methods of cooking that have been passed down through generations, preserving the flavors and techniques that define this unique culinary heritage. Central to Maori cuisine is the hangi, a traditional earth oven method that brings people together in a celebration of food, community, and culture.

The origins of Maori cuisine can be traced back to the arrival of Polynesian ancestors who settled in New Zealand over a millennium ago. These early settlers brought with them staple foods such as kumara (sweet potato), taro, and yams, adapting their agricultural practices to the new environment. Over time, they incorporated native ingredients into their diet, including fish, shellfish, birds, and various plants, creating a diverse and sustainable food system.

The hangi is perhaps the most iconic aspect of Maori culinary tradition. This ancient method of cooking involves digging a pit in the ground, where food is placed on heated stones and covered with earth to trap the heat and steam. The process begins with the selection of suitable stones, typically volcanic rocks that can withstand high temperatures without cracking. These stones are heated in a fire until they glow red, a crucial step that ensures the food is cooked evenly.

Once the stones are ready, they are carefully arranged in the pit, and the food is placed on top. Traditionally, the ingredients include a variety of meats such as pork, lamb, and chicken, along with root vegetables like kumara, potatoes, and pumpkin. The food is typically wrapped in leaves or placed in wire baskets to prevent direct contact with the stones and soil. Finally, the pit is covered with layers of wet cloths or leaves, followed by soil to seal in the heat and steam. This slow-cooking process can take several hours, allowing the flavors to meld and the food to become tender and infused with the earthy aroma of the hangi.

The hangi is more than just a cooking technique; it is a social event that brings communities together. Preparing a hangi requires collaboration and coordination, with each person contributing to the process. It is an opportunity for storytelling, sharing knowledge, and strengthening bonds within the community. The anticipation builds as the earth is removed, revealing the feast beneath, and the aroma that fills the air is a testament to the labor and love that went into its creation.

While the hangi remains a cherished tradition, Maori cuisine has evolved over time, incorporating new ingredients and influences. The arrival of Europeans introduced a variety of foods such as pork, potatoes, and wheat, which were integrated into Maori cooking practices. Today, Maori chefs and home cooks continue to innovate, blending traditional techniques with contemporary flavors to create dishes that honor their heritage while embracing modern tastes.

Seafood holds a special place in Maori cuisine, reflecting the proximity of Maori communities to the coast and their reliance on the ocean's resources. Fish such as snapper, kahawai, and tarakihi are commonly caught and prepared using methods like smoking, drying, and baking. Shellfish, including mussels, paua (abalone), and pipis, are often gathered by hand and enjoyed fresh or cooked in a variety of dishes. The preparation of kaimoana (seafood) is often accompanied by rituals and customs that demonstrate respect for the ocean and its bounty.

Native plants also play a significant role in Maori cuisine, contributing unique flavors and nutritional benefits. The leaves of the kawakawa plant, for example, are used to season foods and are believed to have medicinal properties. The pikopiko fern, with its tender young fronds, is a sought-after delicacy, often served as a vegetable side dish. The berries of the karaka tree, once carefully prepared to remove toxins, provide a starchy, nutty addition to meals.

Modern Maori cuisine is a vibrant fusion of traditional and contemporary elements, showcased in a range of settings from family gatherings to fine dining establishments. Chefs like Monique Fiso and Rex Morgan are at the forefront of this culinary renaissance, creating dishes that celebrate indigenous ingredients and techniques. Through their innovative approaches, they are bringing Maori flavors to a wider audience, both in New Zealand and internationally.

Efforts to preserve and promote Maori cuisine are supported by initiatives such as food festivals, cooking workshops, and cultural exchanges. These events provide a platform for Maori chefs, artisans, and food producers to share their knowledge and passion, fostering appreciation and understanding of this rich culinary heritage. Educational programs also play a crucial role, teaching younger generations about traditional foods and cooking methods, ensuring that these practices endure.

In recent years, there has been a growing recognition of the importance of sustainable and ethical food practices within Maori communities. The principles of kaitiakitanga, or guardianship, guide the approach to resource management, emphasizing respect for the environment and the responsibility to protect it for future generations. This ethos is reflected in the way food is sourced, prepared, and shared, reinforcing the connection between people, land, and food.

Maori cuisine, with its deep-rooted traditions and evolving influences, offers a unique perspective on the relationship between culture and food. It is a testament to the resilience and adaptability of the Maori people, who have maintained their culinary heritage while embracing change. Through the flavors and stories of their food, the Maori invite others to experience the richness of their culture and the warmth of their hospitality.

As you explore Maori cuisine, you are not only tasting the flavors of the land but also engaging with the history and values of its people. Each dish is a reminder of the connections that bind us to our ancestors, the environment, and each other. By honoring these traditions and sharing them with the world, the Maori continue to celebrate their identity and contribute to the diverse tapestry of global cuisine.

4. Sacred Sites and Legends

The landscape of New Zealand is steeped in mystery and reverence, where the sacred sites of the Maori people are woven with legends that echo through time. These sites are not merely geographical locations but are imbued with spiritual significance and cultural heritage. They serve as living connections to ancestors and the divine, providing insight into the beliefs and traditions that have shaped Maori identity for centuries.

One of the most revered sacred sites is the mountain Aoraki, known to many as Mount Cook. According to Maori legend, Aoraki was the eldest son of Rakinui, the Sky Father. Alongside his brothers, Aoraki embarked on a journey through the heavens in a celestial canoe. When the canoe overturned, the brothers climbed onto its side, eventually transforming into the mountains of the South Island. Aoraki, the tallest, became the towering peak that bears his name, standing as a testament to the enduring bond between the land and its people. For the Ngai Tahu iwi, Aoraki is not just a mountain but a revered ancestor, embodying the spirit and authority of their lineage.

In the North Island, Lake Taupo's vast expanse holds both natural beauty and mythological depth. Formed by a massive volcanic eruption nearly two millennia ago, the lake is the heart of stories involving Tia and Ngatoroirangi, explorers who journeyed through the region. Ngatoroirangi, a tohunga or priest, is celebrated for his quest to bring geothermal warmth to the land. When he struggled against the cold on Mount Tongariro, his prayers reached his sisters in Hawaiki, who sent fire demons to his aid. This act of divine intervention is believed to have created the geothermal wonders that dot the landscape around Lake Taupo, linking the environment to the spiritual realm.

The Waitomo Caves, renowned for their glowworm displays, are another site where natural wonder and legend intersect. These limestone caves are said to be home to the taniwha, mythical creatures that inhabit deep waters and caves. Maori stories often portray taniwha as guardians of their domains, capable of both benevolent protection and fearsome power. The glowworms, lighting up the darkness with their ethereal glow, add an otherworldly dimension to the caves, reinforcing their mystical reputation. Visitors to Waitomo are reminded of the respect owed to these ancient dwellings and the creatures that reside within them.

Cape Reinga, at the northernmost tip of the North Island, serves as a poignant symbol of the Maori connection to the afterlife. Known in Maori as Te Rerenga Wairua, it is regarded as the departing place for spirits journeying to their ancestral homeland of Hawaiki. According to legend, the spirits of the deceased travel through the roots of an ancient pohutukawa tree that clings to the cliffs, descending into the ocean to begin their voyage. This site is a place of reflection and reverence, where the living can feel the presence of their ancestors and the continuity of life beyond death.

The volcanic plateau of Rotorua, with its geothermal activity and vibrant Maori culture, is a hub of sacred sites and stories. The Pink and White Terraces, once considered the eighth wonder of the natural world, were a spectacular geothermal formation that tragically vanished in the eruption of Mount Tarawera in 1886. The eruption itself has become part of local lore, with tales of a phantom canoe appearing on Lake Tarawera as a portent of the impending disaster. Although the terraces are lost, the legacy of their beauty and the stories surrounding them endure, contributing to Rotorua's rich tapestry of legend and spirituality.

The Waipoua Forest, home to the mighty kauri tree Tane Mahuta, embodies the deep reverence the Maori have for the natural world. Named after the god of the forest, Tane Mahuta is estimated to be over a thousand years old and is the largest known living kauri tree. For the Maori, Tane Mahuta is not only a physical marvel but a living ancestor, representing the life-giving force of the forest and its role as a cradle of life. The forest itself is sacred, a reminder of the interconnectedness of all living things and the duty of stewardship that comes with this understanding.

The legends surrounding these sacred sites are more than stories; they are teachings that convey the values and principles of Maori culture. They emphasize the themes of respect, guardianship, and the enduring presence of the ancestors. These narratives serve as guides for living in harmony with the environment and maintaining the balance between the physical and spiritual worlds.

In preserving these sacred sites, the Maori uphold their cultural heritage and affirm their identity. This preservation is not without challenges, as modern pressures such as tourism and development can threaten the sanctity of these places. However, efforts are underway to ensure that the sacred sites are protected and respected. Collaborative initiatives between Maori communities, government agencies, and conservation groups aim to balance the needs of cultural preservation with those of economic and environmental sustainability.

Educational programs and cultural experiences play a vital role in fostering understanding and respect for Maori sacred sites and legends. By sharing these stories and their significance with visitors and younger generations, the Maori continue to keep their traditions alive. These efforts help cultivate appreciation for the cultural richness of New Zealand and the unique perspectives it offers.

The sacred sites and legends of the Maori are an integral part of the nation's identity, offering a glimpse into the spiritual and cultural foundations of its indigenous people. They remind us of the profound connections between land, people, and the divine, inviting us to reflect on our own place within this intricate web of relationships. Through the stories and sites that have been passed down through generations, the Maori ensure that their heritage is celebrated and cherished, both now and in the future.

5. Maori Language and Phrases

The Maori language, known as Te Reo Maori, is a cornerstone of Maori identity and culture. It embodies the history, values, and worldview of the Maori people, serving as a vital link between generations. In recent years, there has been a significant resurgence in the use and appreciation of Te Reo, driven by efforts to preserve and revitalize this indigenous language. For those interested in learning Te Reo, it offers not only linguistic skills but also a deeper understanding of Maori culture and perspectives.

Te Reo Maori is a Polynesian language closely related to others in the Pacific, such as Hawaiian, Tahitian, and Rapa Nui. Its structure and vocabulary reflect the unique environment and lifestyle of the Maori people. Traditionally, Te Reo was an oral language, with knowledge and stories passed down through generations by word of mouth. This oral tradition remains central to Maori culture, with many songs, chants, and oratory practices still widely used today.

Learning Te Reo Maori begins with understanding its phonetic structure and pronunciation. The language consists of five vowel sounds—A, E, I, O, and U—each pronounced consistently, much like the vowels in Spanish. Consonants include H, K, M, N, P, R, T, W, NG, and WH, with the latter two having distinctive sounds: "NG" as in "sing," and "WH" often pronounced as an "f" sound. Mastering these sounds is crucial, as pronunciation holds great importance in conveying meaning accurately.

Greetings and basic phrases are fundamental to engaging with Te Reo Maori. The most common greeting, "Kia ora," is versatile, used to say hello, thank you, or express agreement. It's a simple yet powerful phrase that embodies the essence of well-being and connection. Another important greeting is "Tēnā koe," which is used to acknowledge one person formally, while "Tēnā kōrua" and "Tēnā koutou" address two or more people, respectively. Understanding these variations is essential for showing respect and etiquette in different social contexts.

Introducing oneself in Maori often involves sharing one's whakapapa, or genealogy. A typical introduction might begin with "Ko [name] tōku ingoa," meaning "My name is [name]." This can be followed by information about one's ancestry and connections, such as "Ko [mountain] te maunga" (My mountain is [name]) and "Ko [river] te awa" (My river is [name]). These phrases reflect the Maori belief in the interconnectedness of people and the natural world, grounding identity in place and heritage.

Expressions of gratitude and politeness are integral to Te Reo Maori. "Ngā mihi" (thank you) and "Aroha mai" (excuse me) are commonly used to show appreciation and consideration. The concept of aroha, often translated as love or compassion, is a guiding principle in Maori culture, emphasizing the importance of empathy and kindness in interactions.

Te Reo Maori also includes a wealth of proverbs, or whakataukī, that encapsulate wisdom and cultural values. These sayings often draw on imagery from nature and emphasize the importance of community, resilience, and humility. For example, "He aha te mea nui o te ao? He tangata, he tangata, he tangata," translates to "What is the most important thing in the world? It is people, it is people, it is people." Such proverbs offer insights into the Maori worldview and serve as a reminder of the values that underpin Maori society.

Incorporating Te Reo Maori into everyday life can be both rewarding and enriching. For beginners, starting with simple phrases and greetings is an accessible way to build confidence and familiarity with the language. Engaging with Maori media, such as television programs, radio stations, and online resources, can also provide valuable exposure to the language in context. Many communities offer language classes and workshops, providing opportunities for immersive learning and practice.

The revitalization of Te Reo Maori has been supported by legislative and educational initiatives. The Maori Language Act of 1987 recognized Te Reo as an official language of New Zealand, paving the way for its inclusion in schools, government, and media. The establishment of Kohanga Reo (language nests) and Kura Kaupapa Maori (Maori immersion schools) has been instrumental in fostering bilingual education and ensuring that future generations grow up fluent in both Maori and English.

Te Wiki o Te Reo Maori, or Maori Language Week, is an annual celebration that promotes the use and appreciation of Te Reo across the country. During this week, events and activities encourage people of all backgrounds to engage with the language, fostering a sense of shared cultural heritage and pride. This celebration highlights the importance of language as a living, evolving entity, capable of adapting to contemporary contexts while honoring its roots.

For learners of Te Reo Maori, persistence and practice are key. The journey of language learning is one of gradual progress and discovery, where each new word and phrase deepens one's connection to the culture. It's important to embrace mistakes as part of the learning process, seeking guidance from fluent speakers and participating in language communities that offer support and encouragement.

The resurgence of Te Reo Maori is a testament to the resilience and determination of the Maori people to preserve their linguistic heritage. By learning and using Te Reo, individuals contribute to the revitalization of the language, ensuring its continuity and vibrancy for future generations. Moreover, engaging with Te Reo opens the door to a deeper appreciation of Maori culture, fostering mutual respect and understanding in an increasingly diverse society.

Through the language, learners gain access to a rich tapestry of stories, traditions, and perspectives that inform the Maori way of life. Te Reo Maori is not merely a means of communication; it is a vessel of cultural identity, carrying the legacy of the ancestors and the wisdom of the land. In embracing Te Reo, one embarks on a journey of cultural exchange and personal growth, contributing to the ongoing narrative of New Zealand's unique cultural landscape.

CHAPTER 3: AUCKLAND AND THE NORTH ISLAND

1. Highlights of Auckland

Auckland, often referred to as the "City of Sails," is a vibrant metropolis that uniquely blends urban sophistication with natural beauty. Nestled between two harbors, it offers a diverse array of experiences that make it a standout destination on the North Island of New Zealand. From its breathtaking landscapes and unique cultural offerings to its bustling city life, Auckland provides an enchanting introduction for anyone eager to explore the North Island.

The iconic Sky Tower dominates Auckland's skyline, rising 328 meters above the city. It offers panoramic views that stretch as far as the eye can see, providing a perfect vantage point to appreciate Auckland's stunning geography. Visitors can enjoy fine dining in the revolving restaurant or take on the SkyWalk and SkyJump for a thrilling adventure. The tower is not just a landmark but a symbol of the city's dynamic spirit and modernity.

Auckland's waterfront is a lively hub of activity and a must-visit for any traveler. The Viaduct Harbour, once a commercial wharf, has been transformed into a vibrant precinct filled with restaurants, bars, and cafes. It's a place where locals and visitors alike gather to enjoy the maritime atmosphere, watch yachts glide by, and savor fresh seafood. The nearby Wynyard Quarter, with its contemporary architecture and public spaces, further enhances the waterfront experience, offering a glimpse into the city's commitment to sustainable urban development.

The city's multicultural essence is reflected in its diverse neighborhoods, each offering its own unique flavor. Ponsonby, known for its trendy cafes, boutique shops, and vibrant nightlife, is a favorite among those seeking a taste of Auckland's creative scene. The historic suburb of Parnell, with its charming Victorian villas and art galleries, provides a more refined experience, while Newmarket is a bustling hub for shopping enthusiasts.

Auckland's commitment to preserving its natural environment is evident in its numerous parks and green spaces. Cornwall Park, with its sprawling lawns and ancient trees, offers a tranquil escape from the city's hustle and bustle. Within the park lies One Tree Hill, a volcanic peak of great cultural significance to the Maori, providing a panoramic view of the city. The Auckland Domain, the city's oldest park, is home to the Auckland War Memorial Museum, which houses an extensive collection of Maori and Pacific artifacts, offering insights into the region's rich history and cultural heritage.

The Maori influence is deeply woven into the fabric of Auckland's identity. The city's name itself, Tāmaki Makaurau, reflects its historical significance as a place of gathering and trade. Visitors can engage with Maori culture through various experiences, such as guided tours at the Auckland Museum, which offer performances of traditional songs and dances, providing a window into the Maori way of life.

Auckland is also a gateway to some of the North Island's most stunning natural attractions. Just a short ferry ride from the city lies Waiheke Island, renowned for its vineyards, olive groves, and pristine beaches. The island's laid-back atmosphere and stunning coastal views make it a popular day trip destination for those seeking relaxation and indulgence. Outdoor enthusiasts can explore the island's walking trails, which wind through native bush and offer spectacular vistas of the Hauraki Gulf.

For those interested in marine life, the nearby Hauraki Gulf Marine Park is a haven for wildlife enthusiasts. The park's waters are home to diverse marine species, including dolphins, whales, and seabirds. Eco-tours provide opportunities for visitors to encounter these creatures in their natural habitat, enhancing their appreciation for New Zealand's unique biodiversity.

Auckland's proximity to the Waitakere Ranges offers another opportunity to connect with nature. This regional park, located just west of the city, boasts lush rainforests, cascading waterfalls, and dramatic coastal views. The park's extensive network of walking tracks caters to all levels of fitness, from leisurely strolls to challenging hikes, allowing visitors to immerse themselves in the tranquility of the native bush.

Culinary delights abound in Auckland, with a dining scene that reflects the city's multicultural character. From high-end restaurants offering innovative cuisine to bustling food markets serving international street food, there's something to satisfy every palate. The city's thriving food scene is celebrated annually during the Auckland Restaurant Month, where food lovers can enjoy special menus and culinary events across the city.

Auckland's arts and culture scene is equally vibrant, with numerous galleries, theaters, and music venues showcasing local and international talent. The Auckland Art Gallery Toi o Tāmaki, with its impressive collection of New Zealand and Pacific art, is a cultural highlight. The city's theaters host a diverse range of performances, from contemporary dance and theater to world-class concerts and festivals, making Auckland a hub for artistic expression.

Transportation within Auckland is convenient and accessible, with an extensive public transport network that includes buses, trains, and ferries. The city's layout makes it easy to explore on foot or by bike, allowing visitors to experience its neighborhoods at their own pace.

In summary, Auckland offers a captivating blend of urban sophistication and natural beauty, making it an ideal starting point for exploring the North Island. Its rich cultural tapestry, stunning landscapes, and vibrant city life create an unforgettable experience for travelers. Whether you're drawn to its culinary scene, cultural experiences, or outdoor adventures, Auckland invites you to discover the essence of New Zealand's North Island.

2. Adventure in the Bay of Islands

The Bay of Islands, a picturesque enclave on the North Island of New Zealand, is a paradise for adventure seekers and nature lovers alike. This stunning region, with its 144 islands scattered across azure waters, offers a wealth of opportunities for exploration and excitement. From thrilling water activities to serene landscapes, the Bay of Islands promises an unforgettable adventure that captures the essence of New Zealand's natural beauty.

Imagine embarking on a journey that begins in Paihia, the vibrant gateway to the Bay of Islands. This charming town serves as the perfect base for exploring the area's myriad attractions. As you stroll along the waterfront, you can feel the anticipation in the air, with boats gently bobbing in the harbor and the distant call of seabirds setting the scene for the adventures that await.

One of the most exhilarating experiences in the Bay of Islands is sailing through its pristine waters. Chartering a yacht or joining a sailing tour allows you to explore hidden coves, remote beaches, and idyllic islands at your own pace. The feeling of the wind in your hair and the sun on your face as you glide across the sea is a liberating experience that brings you closer to nature. Keep an eye out for playful dolphins, often seen frolicking alongside the boats, adding a touch of magic to your voyage.

For those seeking an adrenaline rush, the Bay of Islands offers world-class diving and snorkeling opportunities. The Rainbow Warrior, a sunken Greenpeace vessel, has become an artificial reef teeming with marine life, and exploring its depths is a unique adventure for certified divers. The waters surrounding the islands are home to colorful coral gardens, schools of fish, and, occasionally, the majestic orca. Donning a snorkel and mask, you can immerse yourself in this underwater wonderland, where every glance reveals a new marvel.

Kayaking is another popular way to discover the hidden gems of the Bay of Islands. Paddling through tranquil bays and along rugged coastlines provides a sense of peace and connection with the natural world. You can venture into sea caves, where sunlight dances on the water, or navigate the narrow channels between islands, feeling the gentle sway of the sea beneath you. Kayaking offers a unique perspective on the landscape, allowing you to explore areas inaccessible by larger vessels.

On land, the Bay of Islands offers a wealth of hiking trails that traverse its diverse terrain. The Cape Brett Track is a challenging yet rewarding hike that takes you through lush forests, past dramatic cliffs, and offers breathtaking views of the ocean. The trail culminates at the iconic Cape Brett Lighthouse, standing sentinel over the meeting point of the Pacific Ocean and the Tasman Sea. The sense of accomplishment at reaching this remote location is matched only by the awe-inspiring vistas that greet you.

For a more leisurely experience, the Waitangi Treaty Grounds provide an opportunity to delve into New Zealand's history and Maori culture. As the site where the Treaty of Waitangi was signed in 1840, it holds great significance for the nation. Visitors can explore the beautifully landscaped grounds, visit the Treaty House, and witness cultural performances that bring Maori traditions to life. The Waitangi Treaty Grounds offer a deeper understanding of the country's heritage, enriching your adventure with cultural insights.

Fishing enthusiasts will find the Bay of Islands to be a veritable paradise. The nutrient-rich waters support an abundance of fish species, making it a prime location for both recreational and sport fishing. Whether you're casting a line from the shore or venturing out on a fishing charter, the thrill of the catch is ever-present. Snapper, kingfish, and marlin are just a few of the species that inhabit these waters, and the satisfaction of reeling in a prize fish is unparalleled.

The Bay of Islands is also a haven for birdwatchers, with its diverse ecosystems supporting a wide range of avian species. The islands are home to native birds such as the tui, fantail, and kereru, while the coastal areas attract seabirds like the gannet and petrel. Exploring the islands' walking tracks and coastal paths with binoculars in hand allows you to observe these birds in their natural habitats, each sighting a testament to the region's rich biodiversity.

As the day draws to a close, the Bay of Islands transforms into a serene haven, offering the perfect backdrop for reflection and relaxation. The setting sun casts a golden glow over the water, painting the sky in hues of pink and orange. Whether you're enjoying a leisurely dinner at a waterfront restaurant in Paihia or unwinding on the deck of a yacht, the tranquil beauty of the bay creates a sense of peace and contentment.

The adventure doesn't end with the setting sun. The Bay of Islands offers a unique opportunity to experience the magic of the night sky.

Far from the lights of the city, the stars shine brightly, illuminating the heavens with a breathtaking display of constellations. Stargazing in this pristine environment is a humbling experience, reminding us of the wonders of the universe and our place within it.

The Bay of Islands is a destination that captures the heart and imagination, offering a wealth of adventures for all who visit. Its stunning landscapes, rich marine life, and vibrant culture create a tapestry of experiences that leave a lasting impression. Whether you're seeking thrills on the water, serenity on land, or a deeper connection with New Zealand's heritage, the Bay of Islands promises an unforgettable journey that will inspire and rejuvenate the soul.

3. The Volcanic Wonders of Rotorua

Rotorua, a geothermal wonderland nestled in the heart of New Zealand's North Island, is a place where the earth's raw power and beauty converge. The city is renowned for its geothermal activity, manifesting in bubbling mud pools, steaming vents, and geysers that punctuate the landscape. This unique environment, combined with its rich Maori heritage, makes Rotorua a captivating destination that offers visitors an opportunity to witness the dynamic forces that shape our planet.

The geothermal features of Rotorua are a result of its location on the Pacific Ring of Fire, a seismically active region known for its volcanic activity. The city sits atop a geothermal field that extends for miles, providing a fascinating glimpse into the earth's inner workings. One of the most iconic geothermal attractions in Rotorua is the Pohutu Geyser, located in the Whakarewarewa Thermal Valley. Pohutu, meaning "big splash" in Maori, lives up to its name, erupting up to 20 times a day and reaching heights of 30 meters. The sight of boiling water shooting into the sky is both awe-inspiring and a testament to the geothermal energy that lies beneath the surface.

Adjacent to Pohutu is the Te Puia cultural center, where visitors can immerse themselves in Maori traditions and learn about the significance of geothermal activity to the local iwi, the Te Arawa people. The center offers guided tours that explore the history and cultural importance of the area, showcasing traditional carving, weaving, and the preparation of hangi, a Maori feast cooked using geothermal heat. This cultural experience enriches the understanding of how the Maori have lived in harmony with the geothermal landscape for centuries.

The Wai-O-Tapu Thermal Wonderland is another must-visit geothermal attraction in Rotorua. Known for its vibrant colors and surreal landscapes, Wai-O-Tapu is a natural gallery of geothermal wonders. The Champagne Pool, with its striking orange and turquoise hues, is a highlight, created by deposits of minerals such as arsenic and antimony. Nearby, the Devil's Bath, a fluorescent green pool, offers a striking contrast against the surrounding terrain. These vivid displays are continually shaped by geothermal activity, making each visit to Wai-O-Tapu a unique experience.

For those interested in exploring the geothermal landscape further, Hell's Gate offers a dramatic setting where visitors can witness the earth's raw energy at play. This geothermal park boasts the Southern Hemisphere's largest hot waterfall, Kakahi Falls, as well as boiling mud pools and steaming fumaroles. The mud at Hell's Gate is renowned for its therapeutic properties, and visitors can indulge in a mud bath or sulfur spa, experiencing firsthand the healing benefits that have been utilized by the Maori for generations.

Rotorua's geothermal activity extends beyond its surface features, influencing its natural environment in diverse ways. The city is surrounded by a series of lakes, many of which were formed by volcanic eruptions. Lake Rotorua, the largest of these, is a caldera lake created by a massive volcanic explosion over 200,000 years ago. The lake's geothermal springs contribute to its unique ecology, supporting a variety of birdlife and providing opportunities for recreational activities such as fishing, boating, and kayaking.

The Okataina Volcanic Centre, located east of Rotorua, is another area of geological interest. This volcanic complex has been the site of several significant eruptions, including the eruption of Mount Tarawera in 1886, which was one of New Zealand's most devastating volcanic events. The eruption destroyed the famed Pink and White Terraces, considered one of the natural wonders of the world, and reshaped the landscape dramatically. Today, the Waimangu Volcanic Valley stands as a testament to the power of that eruption, with its steaming craters, hot springs, and Frying Pan Lake—the world's largest hot spring lake.

The Maori people have long recognized the geothermal activity of Rotorua as a source of energy and sustenance. Geothermal springs have been used for cooking, bathing, and heating, integrating seamlessly into daily life. The Maori concept of kaitiakitanga, or guardianship, underscores the responsibility to protect and preserve these natural resources for future generations. This ethos is reflected in the sustainable management practices employed in Rotorua, ensuring that the geothermal environment remains healthy and vibrant.

Rotorua's geothermal wonders are complemented by its lush forests and scenic landscapes, offering a diverse range of outdoor activities. The Redwoods Whakarewarewa Forest, with its towering California redwoods and extensive network of trails, is a haven for hikers, mountain bikers, and nature enthusiasts. The forest provides a serene contrast to the geothermal activity, with its cool, shaded paths and tranquil atmosphere.

Adventure seekers can also experience the thrill of white-water rafting on the Kaituna River, home to the world's highest commercially rafted waterfall, Tutea Falls. The river's geothermal-fed waters add an element of warmth to the exhilarating rapids, making for a unique rafting experience. For those looking for a more relaxed adventure, the Polynesian Spa offers a chance to unwind in geothermal mineral pools, surrounded by the natural beauty of Lake Rotorua.

Rotorua's volcanic wonders are a testament to the dynamic forces that continue to shape New Zealand's landscape. The interplay between geothermal activity and Maori culture creates a rich tapestry of experiences that highlight the deep connection between people and the land. Whether witnessing the power of a geyser, exploring a volcanic valley, or indulging in a geothermal spa, visitors to Rotorua are invited to discover the extraordinary beauty and vitality of this unique region. The stories and landscapes of Rotorua remind us of the earth's ever-changing nature and our place within its magnificent tapestry.

4. Wine Tasting in Hawke's Bay

Hawke's Bay, a sun-drenched region on New Zealand's North Island, is synonymous with exceptional wine production, celebrated for its vineyards that stretch across rolling hills and fertile plains. This picturesque landscape, framed by the Pacific Ocean to the east and the rugged Ruahine and Kaweka ranges to the west, creates an ideal microclimate for viticulture. Wine enthusiasts flock to Hawke's Bay to indulge in its diverse offerings, ranging from robust reds to crisp whites, making it a premier destination for wine tasting and exploration.

The history of wine production in Hawke's Bay dates back to the mid-19th century, with the establishment of the Mission Estate Winery by French missionaries. This pioneering venture laid the foundation for what would become one of New Zealand's most renowned wine regions. Today, Hawke's Bay boasts over 200 vineyards and more than 70 wineries, each contributing to the region's reputation for producing high-quality wines.

The region's diverse terroir is key to its wine-making success. The combination of warm, sunny days and cool nights, along with a variety of soil types, provides the perfect conditions for growing a wide range of grape varieties. The Gimblett Gravels, an ancient riverbed with gravelly soils, is particularly famous for producing some of the best Bordeaux-style red blends outside of France. The unique soil structure allows for excellent drainage and heat retention, resulting in wines with intense flavors and complexity.

Exploring the vineyards of Hawke's Bay is a sensory journey that engages all the senses. The aroma of fermenting grapes mingles with the earthy scent of the soil, creating an olfactory symphony that is both intoxicating and inviting. As you wander through the rows of vines, the sun casts a warm glow over the landscape, highlighting the vibrant green foliage and the ripening grapes that hang in clusters, ready for harvest.

Wine tasting in Hawke's Bay is an experience that transcends the mere act of sampling different varieties. It's an opportunity to engage with passionate vintners who are eager to share their knowledge and stories. At each winery, you're invited to savor the nuances of flavor that define the region's wines, from the bold and spicy Syrahs to the elegant and aromatic Chardonnays. Each sip reveals the dedication and craftsmanship that goes into creating these exceptional wines, offering a glimpse into the heart and soul of the region.

The art of wine tasting involves more than just the palate; it requires an appreciation for the wine's color, aroma, and texture. As you pour a glass, observe the hue and clarity, noting the subtle variations that suggest the wine's age and grape variety. Swirling the wine in your glass releases its bouquet, allowing you to inhale the complex aromas that hint at the flavors to come. With each sip, let the wine linger on your tongue, discerning the balance of acidity, tannins, and fruit that create its unique profile.

Hawke's Bay is renowned for its red wines, particularly those made from Cabernet Sauvignon, Merlot, and Syrah grapes. These full-bodied wines are characterized by their deep color, rich flavors, and velvety tannins, making them a favorite among red wine aficionados. The region's Bordeaux-style blends, often crafted with precision and care, showcase the harmonious marriage of these grape varieties, resulting in wines that are both powerful and elegant.

While red wines dominate the landscape, Hawke's Bay also excels in producing exceptional white wines. Chardonnay, one of the region's most popular white varietals, is celebrated for its versatility and depth. The cool maritime climate allows for a slow ripening process, resulting in Chardonnays with bright acidity and complex flavors. These wines range from crisp and mineral-driven to rich and buttery, offering something for every palate.

Sauvignon Blanc and Pinot Gris are also prominent in Hawke's Bay, each offering its own unique expression of the region's terroir. Sauvignon Blanc, with its vibrant acidity and tropical fruit notes, captures the essence of the New Zealand style, while Pinot Gris, with its aromatic nose and lush mouthfeel, offers a more subdued yet equally captivating experience.

For those seeking a more immersive experience, many wineries in Hawke's Bay offer guided tours of their vineyards and cellars. These tours provide an in-depth look at the wine-making process, from grape to glass, and offer a behind-the-scenes glimpse into the artistry and science involved in crafting each bottle. Walking through the vineyards, you gain an appreciation for the meticulous care that goes into nurturing the vines throughout the seasons, each step crucial in the journey from vine to wine.

Pairing wine with food is another highlight of the Hawke's Bay wine-tasting experience. The region's fertile land supports a bounty of fresh produce, seafood, and artisanal products that complement the wines perfectly. Many wineries feature on-site restaurants or cafes that showcase the best local ingredients, creating dishes that highlight the flavors of the region. Whether it's a sumptuous cheese platter, a succulent lamb dish, or a delicate seafood creation, these culinary delights enhance the wine-tasting journey, offering a feast for the senses.

Hawke's Bay's wine festivals and events are a celebration of the region's vibrant wine culture. The annual Hawke's Bay Wine Auction, one of New Zealand's most prestigious wine events, attracts wine lovers and collectors from around the world. Other events, such as the F.A.W.C! (Food and Wine Classic) and the Harvest Hawke's Bay Festival, offer opportunities to indulge in the region's finest wines and culinary offerings, set against the backdrop of stunning landscapes.

Beyond the wine, Hawke's Bay offers a wealth of attractions and activities for visitors to enjoy. The Art Deco architecture of Napier, the region's largest city, provides a charming and unique backdrop for exploration. The nearby Te Mata Peak offers panoramic views of the surrounding countryside, while the coastal trails and beaches invite relaxation and outdoor adventure. Whether you're cycling through the vineyards, exploring local art galleries, or simply soaking in the natural beauty, Hawke's Bay offers a diverse array of experiences that complement its wine-tasting offerings.

In Hawke's Bay, wine tasting is more than just an activity—it's a journey into the heart of a region where nature, culture, and passion converge. Each visit to a vineyard is an opportunity to connect with the land, the people, and the stories that shape this remarkable wine region. As you savor each glass, you're not just tasting the flavors of the wine; you're experiencing the essence of Hawke's Bay itself—a place where the art of winemaking is woven into the fabric of the land and its people.

5. Exploring Wellington's Cultural Scene

Wellington, the capital city of New Zealand, is a vibrant cultural hub that captivates visitors with its dynamic arts scene, rich history, and eclectic mix of influences. Nestled between a picturesque harbor and rolling hills, Wellington offers an array of cultural experiences that reflect its status as the nation's creative heart. From world-class museums and galleries to innovative theater and music, the city is a treasure trove for anyone eager to explore its artistic and cultural offerings.

The city's compact size makes it easy to navigate, with many of its cultural attractions located within walking distance of each other. A stroll through Wellington's streets reveals a city that embraces creativity and diversity. The colorful murals that adorn the walls of buildings hint at the city's commitment to public art, while the buzzing cafes and boutique shops reflect its cosmopolitan flair.

A cornerstone of Wellington's cultural scene is Te Papa Tongarewa, the Museum of New Zealand. This national museum offers an immersive journey through the country's history, art, and natural environment. Its innovative, interactive exhibits engage visitors of all ages, providing insights into New Zealand's indigenous Maori culture, colonial past, and unique biodiversity. Highlights include the colossal squid exhibit, the Treaty of Waitangi display, and the stunning Maori art collections. Te Papa is more than a museum; it's a space where stories come alive, inviting visitors to engage with the rich tapestry of New Zealand's heritage.

Art enthusiasts will find Wellington's gallery scene equally compelling. The City Gallery Wellington, located in the heart of Civic Square, showcases contemporary art from New Zealand and around the world. Its rotating exhibitions feature works by both established and emerging artists, challenging viewers to contemplate diverse themes and perspectives. The gallery's commitment to fostering dialogue and creativity makes it a vital part of the city's cultural landscape.

Wellington's theater scene is another highlight, offering a diverse range of performances that cater to all tastes. The iconic St. James Theatre, with its ornate architecture and rich history, hosts everything from musicals and ballet to international concerts and comedy shows. Meanwhile, BATS Theatre champions experimental and innovative productions, providing a platform for emerging talent and new ideas. The city's thriving theater community ensures that there's always something engaging happening on stage, from classical plays to cutting-edge contemporary works.

Music is an integral part of Wellington's cultural identity, with a vibrant live music scene that spans genres and styles. The city's numerous bars and venues offer everything from rock and jazz to electronic and indie performances. The annual New Zealand Festival of the Arts, held in Wellington, attracts world-class musicians and performers, transforming the city into a hub of artistic celebration. Whether you're enjoying an intimate acoustic set or dancing to a high-energy DJ, Wellington's music scene offers a soundtrack to the city's creative spirit.

Wellington's film industry is another facet of its cultural allure. Known as the "Coolest Little Capital in the World," it has earned a reputation as a center for film production, thanks in part to the success of the Lord of the Rings and Hobbit trilogies. The Weta Workshop, located in nearby Miramar, offers tours that provide a behind-the-scenes look at the world of movie magic. Visitors can explore the creative process behind some of cinema's most iconic visual effects and props, gaining an appreciation for the artistry and innovation that define Wellington's film industry.

The capital's cultural scene is not limited to indoor venues; it extends into the streets and public spaces. The Wellington Waterfront, with its scenic views and lively atmosphere, hosts numerous festivals and events throughout the year. From the CubaDupa street festival, which celebrates the eclectic spirit of Cuba Street with music, dance, and art, to the Wellington Jazz Festival, the city's outdoor events showcase its creative energy and community spirit.

Wellington's culinary scene is a cultural experience in itself, reflecting the city's diverse influences and creative flair. The city's vibrant food markets, such as the Harbourside Market and the Night Market, offer a taste of Wellington's culinary diversity, with stalls serving everything from traditional Maori hangi to international street food. The city's cafes and restaurants are known for their emphasis on fresh, local ingredients and innovative flavors, making dining in Wellington a delightful adventure.

For those interested in exploring Maori culture further, Wellington offers several opportunities to engage with indigenous traditions and stories. The Wellington City and Sea Museum, located on the waterfront, provides insights into the city's maritime history and Maori heritage. The nearby Zealandia Ecosanctuary, while primarily a conservation project, also offers guided tours that highlight the cultural significance of the land to the Maori people, providing a holistic understanding of the region's natural and cultural history.

Wellington's commitment to sustainability and environmental consciousness is evident in its cultural scene as well. The city has embraced eco-friendly practices in its arts and cultural events, from promoting zero-waste festivals to supporting sustainable design and production methods. This commitment extends to its public transport system, which is efficient and environmentally friendly, making it easy for visitors to explore the city's cultural attractions without leaving a heavy carbon footprint.

In Wellington, culture is not just something to observe; it's something to participate in. The city's open-minded and inclusive atmosphere encourages creativity and self-expression, inviting both locals and visitors to engage with its cultural offerings. Whether you're exploring a gallery, attending a live performance, or simply enjoying the vibrant street art, Wellington's cultural scene offers a wealth of experiences that inspire and captivate. It's a city where creativity thrives, and where the arts are celebrated as an integral part of the community's identity.

6. Hidden Gems of Northland

Northland, the northernmost region of New Zealand, is a land of captivating beauty and cultural richness, often overshadowed by its more famous neighbors. Yet, within its lush landscapes and along its rugged coastlines lie hidden gems waiting to be discovered. These treasures, tucked away from the usual tourist paths, offer a glimpse into the region's unique charm and allure. From secluded beaches to ancient forests, Northland invites you on a journey of exploration and wonder.

One of Northland's most enchanting hidden gems is the Waipoua Forest, home to the majestic Kauri trees. These ancient giants, some over 2,000 years old, stand as silent witnesses to the passage of time. The most famous among them is Tane Mahuta, or "Lord of the Forest," the largest known Kauri tree in the world. As you walk through the forest, the dappled sunlight filtering through the canopy creates a serene atmosphere, and the earthy scent of the forest floor envelops you. The experience is both humbling and awe-inspiring, offering a deep connection to nature and the land's history.

Venturing further along the west coast, you'll find the Hokianga Harbour, a hidden gem that exudes tranquility and charm. This natural harbor, with its golden sand dunes and calm waters, is steeped in Maori legend and history. It is said to be the landing place of Kupe, the legendary Polynesian navigator who discovered New Zealand. The small towns dotting the harbor, such as Opononi and Rawene, offer a glimpse into the laid-back lifestyle of Northland's coastal communities. Exploring the harbor by kayak or ferry provides a unique perspective on its beauty, with the ever-changing light reflecting off the water and casting a magical glow over the landscape.

The east coast of Northland is equally captivating, with its pristine beaches and hidden coves. One such gem is Matapouri Bay, a secluded beach known for its crystal-clear waters and powdery white sand. Nearby, the Mermaid Pools, natural rock pools filled with turquoise water, offer a secluded spot for a refreshing swim. The sense of peace and isolation found here is a stark contrast to the bustling tourist spots further south, providing a perfect escape into nature's embrace.

Further south lies the Whangarei Heads, a rugged peninsula offering breathtaking views and outdoor adventures. The area is home to a network of walking trails that traverse its diverse landscapes, from coastal cliffs to lush native bush. The climb to the summit of Mount Manaia is rewarded with panoramic views of the harbor and surrounding islands, a sight that leaves a lasting impression on all who venture there. The Whangarei Heads are also a haven for wildlife, with opportunities to spot native birds and marine life along the coast.

Northland's hidden gems are not limited to natural wonders; its cultural heritage is equally rich and intriguing. The Waitangi Treaty Grounds, while a well-known historical site, holds lesser-known stories and insights into New Zealand's past. The museum and cultural performances offer a deeper understanding of the Treaty of Waitangi, New Zealand's founding document, and the complex relationship between Maori and European settlers. Engaging with these stories provides a nuanced perspective on the region's history and its ongoing significance.

In the heart of Northland lies the Bay of Islands, a region known for its stunning beauty and maritime history. While popular with tourists, it still harbors hidden treasures away from the crowds. The small town of Russell, once known as the "Hell Hole of the Pacific" for its rowdy past, now exudes charm and tranquility. Its historic buildings, quaint cafes, and art galleries invite leisurely exploration. A short ferry ride away, the island of Urupukapuka offers secluded beaches and walking trails with breathtaking views of the surrounding islands.

Exploring Northland's hidden gems is not complete without sampling the region's culinary delights. The fertile land and abundant coastline provide a bounty of fresh produce and seafood, celebrated in local markets and restaurants. The Matakana Farmers' Market, though slightly south of traditional Northland, is a must-visit for its vibrant atmosphere and array of artisanal products. From freshly shucked oysters to creamy cheeses and local wines, the flavors of Northland offer a taste of the region's richness and diversity.

The journey through Northland's hidden gems is one of discovery and connection, revealing the essence of a region often overlooked. Its natural beauty, cultural heritage, and warm hospitality invite you to linger, to explore, and to embrace the slower pace of life. Whether you find yourself wandering through ancient forests, relaxing on a secluded beach, or engaging with the stories of the past, Northland offers a unique and enriching experience that lingers long after you depart. As you uncover these treasures, you'll come to appreciate the depth and diversity of this remarkable corner of the world, where each hidden gem adds a new dimension to the tapestry of Northland's allure.

CHAPTER 4: THRILLING OUTDOOR ESCAPES

1. Hiking the Tongariro Alpine Crossing

Hiking the Tongariro Alpine Crossing is an adventure that promises both physical challenge and unparalleled beauty. This iconic trek, situated within the Tongariro National Park in New Zealand's central North Island, is renowned as one of the world's best day hikes. Spanning approximately 19.4 kilometers, the trail traverses a dramatic volcanic landscape, offering a unique glimpse into the geological forces that have shaped this region over millennia. As you embark on this journey, you'll encounter breathtaking vistas, vibrant emerald lakes, and rugged volcanic terrain, each element contributing to an unforgettable experience.

The journey begins at Mangatepopo Valley, where the well-marked trail leads hikers through an ancient landscape shaped by past eruptions. Early morning is the ideal time to start, as the cool air and soft light enhance the ethereal beauty of the surroundings. The initial stretch is relatively gentle, providing an opportunity to acclimate to the alpine environment and take in the sweeping views of Mount Tongariro and Mount Ngauruhoe, the latter famously known as "Mount Doom" from the Lord of the Rings films.

As the trail progresses, it gradually ascends towards the Soda Springs, a picturesque waterfall that serves as a natural rest stop. Here, the landscape begins to reveal more of its volcanic character, with rocky outcrops and hardy alpine vegetation dotting the terrain. The climb becomes steeper as you approach the aptly named Devil's Staircase, a challenging section that requires careful footing and steady determination. The ascent is rewarded with increasingly spectacular views, as the surrounding peaks and valleys unfold in all their grandeur.

Upon reaching the South Crater, a vast, flat expanse surrounded by towering ridges, hikers are treated to a sense of awe and solitude. The crater's barren beauty, accentuated by the distant rumble of geothermal activity, creates an otherworldly atmosphere. It's a reminder of nature's raw power and the ever-changing landscape formed by volcanic forces.

Continuing on, the trail ascends the Red Crater, the highest point of the crossing. This section demands caution, particularly in adverse weather conditions, as the loose scree underfoot can be treacherous. However, the effort is rewarded with a panoramic view of the Red Crater's vivid hues, contrasting sharply with the surrounding landscape. The crater's striking colors, a result of mineral deposits and volcanic activity, offer a visual feast that captivates and inspires.

Descending from the Red Crater, hikers are greeted by the mesmerizing sight of the Emerald Lakes. These vibrant pools, filled with turquoise water, owe their striking color to dissolved minerals from the surrounding geothermal area. The contrast between the lakes' vivid hues and the stark volcanic terrain is nothing short of breathtaking, creating a scene that feels both surreal and serene. It's an ideal spot to pause, reflect, and capture the beauty of the natural world.

The trail continues past the Central Crater and Blue Lake, each offering its own unique charm and allure. The Blue Lake, sacred to the Maori people, is a serene body of water that invites quiet contemplation. Its calm surface reflects the sky and surrounding peaks, creating a tranquil oasis amidst the rugged landscape.

As you descend towards the Ketetahi Hut, the landscape begins to transition from volcanic desolation to lush native bush. The trail meanders through tussock fields and subalpine forest, offering glimpses of the vibrant flora and fauna that thrive in this diverse environment. The gentle descent provides a welcome respite for weary legs, allowing hikers to savor the final stretch of the journey.

Reaching the Ketetahi car park marks the end of the Tongariro Alpine Crossing, a journey that leaves a lasting impression on all who undertake it. The sense of accomplishment, coupled with the memories of the stunning landscapes encountered along the way, creates a profound connection to the natural world and its awe-inspiring beauty.

Preparation is key to a successful hike on the Tongariro Alpine Crossing. Given the alpine environment, weather conditions can change rapidly, requiring hikers to be well-prepared with appropriate gear and clothing. Sturdy hiking boots, layered clothing, a waterproof jacket, and sun protection are essential, along with plenty of water and energy-rich snacks to sustain you throughout the day.

Safety should be a top priority, and it's important to check the weather forecast before setting out. In winter months, the trail may be covered in snow and ice, making it suitable only for experienced hikers with appropriate equipment. During these times, guided tours are recommended to ensure a safe and enjoyable experience.

Respecting the natural environment is paramount, as the Tongariro Alpine Crossing traverses a fragile and sacred landscape. The Maori people hold the area in high regard, and hikers are encouraged to tread lightly, stay on designated paths, and adhere to the principles of Leave No Trace. By doing so, we can help preserve this remarkable landscape for future generations to enjoy.

Hiking the Tongariro Alpine Crossing is more than just a physical challenge; it's an opportunity to connect with one of New Zealand's most stunning natural environments. The journey offers a rare chance to witness the raw beauty and power of a volcanic landscape, while also reflecting on the delicate balance between nature and humanity. For those who embark on this adventure, the memories forged on the trail will endure long after the journey has ended, a testament to the timeless allure of the Tongariro Alpine Crossing.

2. Exploring the Waitomo Glowworm Caves

The Waitomo Glowworm Caves, nestled in the lush landscapes of New Zealand's North Island, offer an enchanting experience that captivates visitors with their otherworldly beauty. These subterranean wonders, formed over millions of years, are home to the luminescent glowworms, Arachnocampa luminosa, a species unique to New Zealand. The caves' mesmerizing glow and intricate formations create a magical atmosphere that draws explorers from around the globe.

As you approach Waitomo, the rolling hills and verdant pastures paint a serene picture of rural New Zealand. The caves, hidden beneath this tranquil landscape, invite you into a world where nature's artistry takes center stage. The journey begins at the Waitomo Glowworm Caves Visitor Centre, where knowledgeable guides provide insights into the caves' history and geology, setting the stage for the adventure that awaits.

The tour begins with a walk through the limestone passages, where stalactites and stalagmites, formed by centuries of mineral deposits, create a dazzling display of natural sculptures. The air is cool and damp, and the sound of dripping water echoes through the caverns, adding to the sense of mystery and wonder. Each step reveals a new perspective on the caves' geological marvels, with formations that resemble delicate curtains, cascading waterfalls, and intricate chandeliers.

The highlight of the Waitomo experience is undoubtedly the boat ride through the Glowworm Grotto. As the guide steers the boat into the cavernous darkness, a hushed silence falls over the group. The only light comes from the gentle glow of thousands of bioluminescent glowworms dotting the ceiling like a starry night sky. This ethereal glow, a result of the glowworms' bioluminescent properties, creates a breathtaking spectacle that leaves a lasting impression.

The glowworms' light is produced through a chemical reaction in their bodies, used to attract prey into their silk threads. This natural wonder is a testament to the ingenuity of nature, showcasing the delicate balance of life within the cave ecosystem. The guides, often locals with deep connections to the area, share stories and legends associated with the caves, adding depth and context to the experience.

Beyond the Glowworm Grotto, the Waitomo region offers a variety of cave systems to explore, each with its own unique features. The Aranui Cave, accessible via a short bush walk, showcases an impressive display of stalactites and stalagmites, set against a backdrop of fossilized coral and seashells. This dry cave offers a contrasting experience to the glowworm caves, with its intricate formations illuminated by strategically placed lighting.

For the more adventurous, the Ruakuri Cave offers a thrilling underground journey that combines walking and black-water rafting. This cave, named after the Maori word for "den of dogs," is rich in both geological and cultural history. The tour begins with a spiral descent through a man-made entrance, leading to an underground labyrinth of limestone formations, glowworms, and hidden waterfalls. The black-water rafting experience, floating through the dark waters on an inner tube, adds an element of excitement and exploration to the cave adventure.

Safety is paramount when exploring the Waitomo caves, and the tours are designed to accommodate various levels of fitness and experience. The guides provide all necessary equipment and instructions, ensuring a safe and enjoyable experience for all visitors. It's important to dress appropriately, with sturdy footwear and warm clothing, as the caves maintain a constant cool temperature year-round.

The Waitomo Glowworm Caves are not only a natural wonder but also a cultural treasure. The caves hold significant importance to the local Maori community, who have been custodians of the land for generations. The name "Waitomo" itself is derived from the Maori words "wai" (water) and "tomo" (hole), reflecting the caves' deep connection to the landscape and its people. This cultural heritage is woven into the fabric of the Waitomo experience, with the guides sharing traditional stories and customs that enrich the understanding of the region's history.

Beyond the caves, the Waitomo district offers a range of attractions and activities that complement the caving experience. The scenic Marokopa Falls, one of New Zealand's most beautiful waterfalls, is a short drive from the caves and provides a stunning backdrop for photography and picnics. The Mangapohue Natural Bridge, a limestone arch carved by the forces of nature, offers a picturesque walk through native bush and farmland, showcasing the region's diverse landscapes.

The Waitomo Caves Discovery Centre, located in the nearby village of Waitomo, offers additional insights into the area's geology and history. Interactive exhibits and displays provide a deeper understanding of the caves' formation, the glowworms' unique biology, and the cultural significance of the region. The center also features a cafe and gift shop, where visitors can relax and reflect on their caving adventures.

The culinary offerings in Waitomo are a delightful surprise, with local cafes and restaurants serving up a taste of New Zealand's fresh produce and flavors. From hearty lamb dishes to fresh seafood and artisanal cheeses, the region's cuisine is a celebration of its agricultural heritage and culinary creativity. Dining in Waitomo provides an opportunity to savor the flavors of the land while sharing stories and experiences from the day's explorations.

Exploring the Waitomo Glowworm Caves is a journey into a world where nature's wonders and cultural heritage come together in a harmonious celebration of beauty and discovery. The experience leaves an indelible mark on all who visit, offering a deeper appreciation for the intricate balance of life beneath the surface. As you emerge from the caves and return to the sunlight, the memories of the glowing grotto and the stories of the land linger, a testament to the timeless allure of Waitomo's subterranean treasures.

3. Surfing Hotspots in Raglan

Raglan, a laid-back coastal town on New Zealand's North Island, is renowned for its legendary surf breaks and vibrant beach culture. Its allure extends beyond the waves, with a creative community and stunning natural landscapes that captivate visitors. For surfers, Raglan is a mecca, offering some of the best surfing conditions in the world, with waves that cater to all levels of expertise.

The journey to Raglan takes you through rolling green hills and pastoral landscapes, setting the stage for the coastal paradise that awaits. As you approach the town, the rhythmic sound of crashing waves serves as a welcoming call to surfers and beachgoers alike. Raglan's surf culture is deeply embedded in its identity, and the town's relaxed vibe reflects the spirit of those who seek solace and exhilaration in the ocean's embrace.

Manu Bay, also known as "The Point," is arguably Raglan's most famous surf break. Internationally acclaimed for its long, peeling left-hand waves, Manu Bay attracts surfers from around the globe. The waves here are consistent, offering rides that can stretch over 500 meters on a good day. This makes it a favorite spot for experienced surfers looking to hone their skills and enjoy the thrill of long rides over the reef. The bay's natural amphitheater provides a perfect vantage point for spectators to watch the action unfold, with surfers carving graceful lines across the waves.

Just around the corner from Manu Bay lies Whale Bay, another iconic surf spot that offers a variety of wave conditions. The waves here are powerful and fast, breaking over a rocky reef that demands respect and skill from those who venture into the lineup. Whale Bay's raw beauty and challenging waves make it a magnet for seasoned surfers seeking adventure and a true test of their abilities. The surrounding landscape, with its dramatic cliffs and native bush, adds to the sense of wild, untamed beauty that defines Raglan's coastline.

For those new to surfing or looking to improve their skills, Ngarunui Beach provides the perfect setting. This expansive sandy beach offers gentle, rolling waves ideal for beginners, as well as surf schools that provide lessons and equipment rentals. The beach's friendly atmosphere and safe conditions make it a welcoming place for families and novice surfers to enjoy the ocean and gain confidence in their abilities. As the sun sets over the horizon, the golden light casts a warm glow over the beach, creating a picturesque scene that captures the essence of Raglan's coastal charm.

Raglan's surf culture extends beyond the water, permeating the town's vibrant community and creative scene. The town is home to a diverse array of artists, musicians, and craftspeople, whose work reflects the natural beauty and laid-back lifestyle of the area. The Raglan Arts Centre and local galleries showcase an eclectic mix of art and crafts, offering visitors a chance to engage with the local creative community and explore the unique expressions of Raglan's cultural identity.

The town itself is a tapestry of eclectic cafes, boutique shops, and colorful street art, each contributing to Raglan's distinctive character. The bustling Raglan Creative Market, held monthly, is a highlight for both locals and visitors, offering a diverse selection of handmade goods, fresh produce, and delicious street food. Here, you can savor the flavors of locally roasted coffee, artisan breads, and fresh seafood, while soaking in the lively atmosphere and community spirit.

For those seeking further adventure, the surrounding region offers a wealth of outdoor activities and natural wonders to explore. The nearby Bridal Veil Falls, a stunning 55-meter waterfall set amidst lush native bush, provides a tranquil escape and a chance to connect with nature. The walking track to the falls is well-maintained and accessible, offering several viewpoints to admire the cascading water and the verdant landscape.

The majestic Mount Karioi, an ancient volcanic peak that stands sentinel over Raglan, beckons hikers and nature enthusiasts to explore its trails. The challenging trek to the summit rewards adventurers with panoramic views of the coast and countryside, a testament to the rugged beauty and diverse landscapes that define the region. The mountain's rich biodiversity, with native birds and flora, adds to the sense of wonder and discovery that accompanies the journey.

Raglan's commitment to sustainability and environmental stewardship is evident in its community initiatives and eco-friendly practices. The town has embraced a culture of conservation, with efforts focused on protecting its natural environment and promoting sustainable living. Local businesses and organizations work together to minimize waste, conserve resources, and educate visitors about the importance of preserving Raglan's unique ecosystems for future generations.

For surfers, Raglan offers more than just world-class waves; it provides a sense of connection to the ocean and a lifestyle that celebrates the harmony between people and nature. The town's welcoming atmosphere and diverse community create a space where individuals can come together to share their passion for surfing and the outdoors. Whether you're carving down the face of a wave at Manu Bay, learning to surf at Ngarunui Beach, or exploring the vibrant town and its surroundings, Raglan offers an experience that resonates deeply with the spirit of adventure and exploration.

In Raglan, the rhythm of the ocean shapes the rhythm of life, inviting you to ride the waves and immerse yourself in the beauty and culture of this remarkable coastal town. The memories forged in its waters and along its shores linger long after you leave, a testament to the enduring allure of Raglan's surfing hotspots and the community that calls them home.

4. Skydiving Over Lake Taupo

Skydiving over Lake Taupo is an exhilarating experience that combines the thrill of freefall with breathtaking views of one of New Zealand's most stunning natural landscapes. Lake Taupo, the largest freshwater lake in Australasia, is nestled in the heart of the North Island, surrounded by snow-capped mountains and lush forests. This unique setting offers skydivers a panoramic vista that is both awe-inspiring and unforgettable.

The adventure begins at Taupo Airport, where a sense of anticipation fills the air. The skydiving center buzzes with excitement as instructors prepare divers for the jump. Whether you're a seasoned skydiver or a first-timer, the team ensures you feel confident and ready for the experience ahead. Safety is paramount, and the briefing covers everything from equipment use to body positioning during freefall, ensuring you're well-prepared for the jump.

As you ascend in the aircraft, the beauty of the region unfolds below. The deep blue expanse of Lake Taupo glimmers in the sunlight, its waters stretching far and wide, bordered by the green hues of native bush. In the distance, the peaks of Tongariro National Park rise majestically, with Mount Ruapehu, Mount Tongariro, and Mount Ngauruhoe standing sentinel over the landscape. This stunning backdrop sets the stage for the thrilling experience to come.

At an altitude of 15,000 feet, the aircraft door opens, and the reality of the jump hits with a rush of adrenaline. For those experiencing tandem skydiving, the comforting presence of an experienced instructor attached to your harness provides reassurance. As you inch towards the edge, the world below seems both vast and intimate, a reminder of the extraordinary experience that skydiving offers.

The moment you exit the plane, gravity takes hold, and you enter freefall. The sensation is unlike any other, a blend of exhilaration and serenity as you hurtle through the sky at speeds of up to 200 kilometers per hour. The wind roars in your ears, yet there's a surreal calmness as the world stretches out beneath you. The freefall lasts approximately 60 seconds, but in that minute, time seems to stand still, and you're fully present in the moment.

At around 5,000 feet, the instructor deploys the parachute, and the transition from freefall to gliding is smooth and gentle. The sudden quiet is striking, and you're left with a sense of peace as you float gracefully through the air. With the parachute open, there's ample time to take in the breathtaking scenery. The vastness of Lake Taupo, with its crystal-clear waters and intricate shoreline, is mesmerizing. The surrounding mountains and forests create a patchwork of colors and textures, a testament to the natural beauty of New Zealand.

As you descend, the instructor guides the parachute with skill and precision, allowing you to savor the descent at a leisurely pace. The perspective from above offers a unique view of the landscape, revealing details that are often hidden from sight. The sensation of floating, coupled with the panoramic views, creates an experience that is both thrilling and meditative, a rare combination that skydiving uniquely provides.

The landing is gentle, and as your feet touch the ground, a rush of emotion and accomplishment washes over you. The exhilaration of freefall, the beauty of the landscape, and the sense of achievement culminate in a moment of pure joy. Skydiving over Lake Taupo is not just about the adrenaline rush; it's about connecting with the environment in a way that few experiences allow, offering both an outer adventure and an inner journey.

For those considering this adventure, it's important to choose a reputable skydiving center with experienced instructors and a strong safety record. The weather plays a crucial role in skydiving, and conditions must be suitable for a safe jump. Instructors monitor weather patterns closely, ensuring that each jump is conducted under optimal conditions. It's advisable to book in advance and remain flexible with timing, as weather can sometimes cause delays or rescheduling.

Dressing appropriately for the jump is essential, with comfortable clothing and secure footwear recommended. The skydiving center provides jumpsuits and all necessary equipment, ensuring you're fully equipped for the experience. Personal cameras are not allowed during the jump for safety reasons, but many centers offer photography and video packages to capture the experience, allowing you to relive the adventure and share it with others.

Skydiving over Lake Taupo is more than just a thrill-seeking activity; it's an opportunity to engage with one of New Zealand's most spectacular regions from a unique perspective. The combination of adrenaline, natural beauty, and personal achievement creates a memory that lasts a lifetime. For those seeking adventure and a deeper connection to the natural world, skydiving over Lake Taupo offers an unparalleled experience that resonates long after the jump is complete.

The adventure doesn't have to end with the skydive; Lake Taupo and its surroundings offer a wealth of activities and attractions to explore. The town of Taupo is vibrant and welcoming, with a range of cafes, restaurants, and shops to enjoy. The geothermal wonders of the region, including hot springs and geysers, provide a relaxing and rejuvenating experience, perfect for unwinding after the excitement of skydiving.

For outdoor enthusiasts, the opportunities are endless. The lake itself offers a range of water-based activities, from kayaking and sailing to fishing and swimming. The nearby Tongariro Alpine Crossing, one of New Zealand's most famous hiking trails, offers a challenging and rewarding trek through volcanic landscapes, providing yet another way to connect with the natural beauty of the region.

Skydiving over Lake Taupo is an experience that defies description, blending the thrill of flight with the serene beauty of New Zealand's landscapes. It's a journey that challenges, inspires, and uplifts, leaving you with a profound sense of wonder and appreciation for the world around you. Whether you're a seasoned adventurer or a curious newcomer, the skies over Lake Taupo offer an invitation to explore, discover, and embrace the extraordinary.

5. Bungee Jumping in Queenstown

Queenstown, often hailed as the adventure capital of the world, offers a thrilling array of activities, with bungee jumping standing out as one of its most iconic experiences. Nestled amidst stunning alpine scenery, this picturesque town on New Zealand's South Island has long been a magnet for adrenaline seekers. The dramatic landscapes of rugged mountains and pristine lakes provide the perfect backdrop for the heart-pounding adventure of bungee jumping.

The journey to Queenstown is itself an adventure, with its winding roads and panoramic views setting the stage for the excitement to come. The town's vibrant atmosphere is palpable, filled with the buzz of adventurers eager to test their limits. Bungee jumping here is not just a leap of faith; it's a rite of passage that leaves an indelible mark on those who dare to take the plunge.

The Kawarau Bridge, located just a short drive from Queenstown, is where commercial bungee jumping was born. This historic site offers a 43-meter jump over the turquoise waters of the Kawarau River, providing a quintessential bungee experience. As you arrive, the sight of the bridge and the river below is both daunting and exhilarating. The anticipation builds as you ascend to the platform, where the experienced staff conducts a thorough safety briefing, ensuring you're prepared for the leap.

Standing on the edge of the bridge, the world seems to hold its breath. The moment before the jump is filled with a mix of fear and excitement, a cocktail of emotions that makes bungee jumping so uniquely captivating. As you take the leap, gravity takes control, and you experience the pure rush of freefall. The sensation is electrifying, a blend of terror and liberation as you plummet towards the river below. The rebound is gentle, and as you bounce back, a wave of euphoria washes over you, accompanied by the realization that you've conquered your fears.

While the Kawarau Bridge offers an iconic jump, Queenstown boasts other equally thrilling bungee sites. The Nevis Bungy, the highest in New Zealand, stands at a staggering 134 meters above the Nevis River. Accessible by a rugged 4WD track and a cable car, the journey to the jump site is an adventure in itself. The Nevis Bungy offers an unparalleled experience, with a longer freefall and a breathtaking view of the surrounding canyon. It's a challenge that attracts both seasoned bungee enthusiasts and those looking to push their boundaries.

For individuals seeking a unique twist on the traditional jump, the Ledge Bungy provides an urban thrill with a spectacular view of Queenstown. Situated 400 meters above the town on Bob's Peak, accessible by gondola, the Ledge offers a freestyle jump that allows you to choose your own jumping style. Whether it's a somersault or a backward leap, the Ledge Bungy encourages creativity, adding a personalized touch to the heart-stopping experience.

Preparation is key to a successful bungee jump, and choosing the right operator is crucial. Queenstown's bungee centers are renowned for their stringent safety standards and experienced staff, ensuring that each jump is conducted safely and professionally. It's important to listen to the instructions given during the briefing and ask questions if you're unsure about any aspect of the jump.

Appropriate attire is essential, with comfortable clothing and secure footwear recommended. Loose items such as jewelry or hats should be removed to prevent any mishaps during the jump. While personal cameras are not allowed on the platform for safety reasons, the operators typically offer photo and video packages, capturing the moment for you to relive and share.

Bungee jumping in Queenstown is more than just an adrenaline rush; it's an opportunity to connect with the stunning natural environment and experience a sense of freedom that is hard to replicate. The combination of breathtaking scenery, expert guidance, and the thrill of the jump creates a memory that resonates long after the experience is over.

For those who prefer to keep their feet on solid ground, Queenstown offers a myriad of other activities and attractions to explore. The town itself is a bustling hub of cafes, restaurants, and shops, providing a lively atmosphere and a chance to unwind after the day's adventures. The local cuisine, with its emphasis on fresh, seasonal produce, offers a culinary journey that complements the town's adventurous spirit.

The surrounding region is a playground for outdoor enthusiasts, with opportunities for hiking, mountain biking, and water sports. The Remarkables and Coronet Peak offer world-class skiing and snowboarding in the winter months, while the crystal-clear waters of Lake Wakatipu invite kayaking, paddleboarding, and scenic cruises. The nearby vineyards of Central Otago provide a chance to sample some of New Zealand's finest wines, offering a more leisurely way to enjoy the region's natural beauty.

Queenstown's history is rich and varied, with a heritage that dates back to the gold rush era. The Lakes District Museum in nearby Arrowtown provides an insight into the area's past, with exhibits that showcase the life and times of the early pioneers. The charming streets of Arrowtown, lined with heritage buildings and boutique shops, offer a glimpse into the region's history, providing a contrast to the modern vibrancy of Queenstown.

Bungee jumping in Queenstown is an experience that transcends the ordinary, offering a blend of adventure, natural beauty, and personal achievement. It's a journey that challenges the spirit, ignites the senses, and leaves an indelible mark on the soul. Whether you're a thrill-seeker looking for your next adrenaline fix or someone seeking to conquer personal fears, the bungee sites of Queenstown offer an invitation to explore the extraordinary and embrace the unknown.

CHAPTER 5: THE SOUTH ISLAND'S SCENIC BEAUTY

1. Discovering Christchurch and Canterbury

Christchurch, known as the Garden City, serves as the gateway to the vast and varied landscapes of the Canterbury region on New Zealand's South Island. As a city that has undergone significant transformation following a series of devastating earthquakes in 2010 and 2011, Christchurch has emerged as a testament to resilience and innovation. It combines charming heritage with contemporary architecture, creating a vibrant urban environment that reflects both its rich history and forward-thinking spirit.

The heart of Christchurch is its city center, where you'll find a mix of historic landmarks and modern developments. The Cathedral Square, once dominated by the iconic ChristChurch Cathedral, now features a blend of new and old, with street performers, market stalls, and art installations creating a lively atmosphere. The transitional Cardboard Cathedral, designed by architect Shigeru Ban, stands as a symbol of hope and creativity, offering a unique space for worship and community gatherings.

The Avon River meanders through the city, providing a picturesque setting for leisurely strolls and punting tours. The riverbanks are lined with beautiful gardens and parks, including the Christchurch Botanic Gardens, a 21-hectare oasis of native and exotic plant species. The gardens offer a tranquil escape from the hustle and bustle, with seasonal displays that showcase the region's diverse flora. Nearby, the Canterbury Museum offers insights into the area's natural and cultural history, with exhibits ranging from Maori artifacts to Antarctic exploration.

Christchurch's food scene is a reflection of its diverse community and commitment to sustainability. The Riverside Market, a bustling hub of artisanal food vendors, offers a taste of local produce and culinary creativity. From freshly caught seafood to gourmet cheeses and handcrafted chocolates, the market is a feast for the senses. The city's cafes and restaurants celebrate local ingredients, with menus that highlight the best of Canterbury's agricultural bounty.

As you venture beyond the city, the Canterbury region unfolds with a dramatic array of landscapes. The Canterbury Plains stretch out towards the Southern Alps, offering a patchwork of farmland, vineyards, and quaint rural towns. The plains are ideal for exploring on a scenic drive or cycling tour, with opportunities to visit local wineries and sample award-winning Pinot Noir and Riesling.

The Southern Alps create a stunning backdrop for outdoor adventures, with activities ranging from hiking and skiing to mountaineering and glacier tours. The Arthur's Pass National Park, located in the heart of the Alps, offers a network of trails that lead through alpine meadows, dense beech forests, and rugged mountain terrain. The park is home to a variety of native wildlife, including the kea, a playful alpine parrot known for its curiosity and intelligence.

Further afield, the coastal town of Akaroa, nestled in the heart of the Banks Peninsula, offers a taste of French-inspired charm and maritime adventure. Founded by French settlers in the 19th century, Akaroa retains its Gallic influence, with charming architecture, cafes, and boutiques lining its streets. The town's harbor is a haven for marine life, including Hector's dolphins, the world's smallest and rarest dolphin species. Eco-cruises and kayaking tours provide opportunities to encounter these playful creatures and explore the peninsula's dramatic coastline.

The Canterbury region is also renowned for its geothermal wonders, with hot springs and thermal pools offering relaxation and rejuvenation. Hanmer Springs, a picturesque alpine village, is famous for its thermal pools and spa, where visitors can soak in mineral-rich waters while surrounded by stunning mountain vistas. The village is a year-round destination, with activities such as hiking, mountain biking, and skiing available in the surrounding forests and peaks.

For those seeking cultural immersion, the region's Maori heritage offers a rich tapestry of history and tradition. The Ngai Tahu, the principal Maori tribe of the South Island, have a deep connection to the land and its resources. Cultural experiences, such as guided tours and traditional performances, provide insights into Maori customs, legends, and way of life. The opportunity to learn about the region's indigenous history enriches the understanding of Canterbury's cultural landscape.

Christchurch and Canterbury are also committed to environmental conservation and sustainability. Initiatives such as native reforestation projects, wildlife preservation programs, and eco-friendly tourism practices reflect the region's dedication to protecting its natural heritage. Visitors are encouraged to engage with these efforts, whether through volunteering, supporting sustainable businesses, or simply adopting responsible travel practices.

In Christchurch and Canterbury, the interplay of nature, culture, and community creates a destination that is both dynamic and deeply rooted in its heritage. Whether you're exploring the urban vibrancy of Christchurch, admiring the breathtaking landscapes of the Canterbury Plains, or immersing yourself in the region's rich cultural tapestry, the experiences here are as diverse as they are rewarding. The journey through Christchurch and Canterbury is one of discovery and connection, offering a glimpse into the heart and soul of New Zealand's South Island.

2. The Majestic Aoraki/Mount Cook

Aoraki/Mount Cook, the tallest peak in New Zealand, stands as a beacon of natural grandeur and cultural significance. Towering at 3,724 meters, this majestic mountain is part of the Southern Alps, a rugged chain of peaks that form the backbone of New Zealand's South Island. Named Aoraki by the Ngāi Tahu, the indigenous Māori people, the mountain holds a revered place in their cultural heritage, symbolizing the ancestral link between the land and its people.

Approaching Aoraki/Mount Cook National Park, the journey itself is a spectacle of changing landscapes. The drive from the nearby town of Twizel winds through the Mackenzie Basin, a vast expanse of tussock grasslands and turquoise lakes. As you draw closer, the snow-capped peaks of the Southern Alps rise dramatically against the sky, culminating in the imposing presence of Aoraki/Mount Cook. This region is a haven for outdoor enthusiasts, offering a myriad of activities that range from serene walks to challenging alpine ascents.

The village of Mount Cook serves as the gateway to the park, providing a base for exploration and adventure. Despite its small size, the village is well-equipped with accommodations, visitor centers, and guiding services that cater to travelers seeking to immerse themselves in the alpine environment. The Sir Edmund Hillary Alpine Centre, named after the legendary mountaineer who honed his skills on these slopes, offers insights into the history and geology of the region, as well as the legacy of exploration and adventure that defines Aoraki/Mount Cook.

For those seeking to experience the mountain up close, the Hooker Valley Track is a must-do. This well-maintained trail offers an accessible yet spectacular hike through the heart of the national park. The track meanders alongside the Hooker River, crossing swing bridges and passing by rushing torrents and alpine meadows. Along the way, you'll encounter icebergs floating in glacial lakes, remnants of the ancient ice flows that shaped this dramatic landscape. The trail culminates at the Hooker Lake, where the reflection of Aoraki/Mount Cook on the water's surface is a sight to behold.

Mountaineers from around the world are drawn to Aoraki/Mount Cook for its challenging climbs and technical ascents. The mountain's rugged terrain and variable weather conditions demand respect and skill, making it a formidable yet rewarding endeavor for experienced climbers. Guided expeditions, led by seasoned alpinists, offer a safe and structured way to tackle the peaks, providing both the expertise and equipment necessary for a successful ascent. The sense of achievement upon reaching the summit, surrounded by the vast expanse of the Southern Alps, is an unparalleled experience that resonates deeply with those who undertake the challenge.

The Tasman Glacier, New Zealand's largest glacier, is another highlight of the region, offering a unique perspective on the glacial landscape. Guided tours provide an opportunity to explore the glacier's icy expanse, either on foot or by boat. Walking on the glacier, with its crevasses and seracs, is an experience that offers both thrill and wonder, revealing the dynamic forces of nature at work. For a bird's-eye view, scenic flights and heli-hikes allow visitors to witness the scale and beauty of the glacier from above, with the added thrill of a helicopter landing on the ice.

Beyond its physical beauty, Aoraki/Mount Cook is also a sanctuary for a diverse range of flora and fauna. The park's unique alpine ecosystem is home to several endemic species, including the kea, a mischievous alpine parrot known for its intelligence and curiosity. The distinctive screech of the kea often accompanies hikers as they traverse the trails, adding an element of lively interaction with the natural world. The park's plant life, adapted to the harsh conditions of the alpine environment, includes a variety of hardy shrubs and delicate wildflowers that create bursts of color against the stark landscape.

The night skies above Aoraki/Mount Cook are equally mesmerizing, offering some of the clearest stargazing opportunities in the southern hemisphere. The region was designated as an International Dark Sky Reserve, recognizing its exceptional quality of starry nights and nocturnal environment. Guided stargazing tours provide telescopes and expert knowledge, allowing visitors to explore the wonders of the universe, from distant galaxies to the glowing band of the Milky Way. The experience of standing beneath a canopy of stars, with the silhouette of Aoraki/Mount Cook in the foreground, is a moment of awe and reflection that connects you to the broader cosmos.

For those interested in the cultural dimensions of Aoraki/Mount Cook, the Ngāi Tahu offer insights into the spiritual significance of the mountain. According to Māori legend, Aoraki was a young boy who, along with his brothers, was transformed into the mountain after their canoe capsized and turned to stone. This story is a cornerstone of Ngāi Tahu identity, underscoring the deep connection between the people and the land. Cultural tours and interpretive programs provide opportunities to learn about these traditions and the Māori worldview, enriching the experience of visiting this sacred landscape.

Aoraki/Mount Cook is more than just a mountain; it is a symbol of natural wonder, cultural heritage, and human endeavor. Whether you're drawn to its peaks for adventure, its trails for exploration, or its stories for inspiration, the mountain offers an experience that is both profound and personal. In the shadow of Aoraki, amidst the grandeur of the Southern Alps, there is a sense of timelessness and majesty that invites reflection and reverence. As you leave this remarkable place, the memory of Aoraki/Mount Cook lingers, a testament to the enduring allure of New Zealand's natural wonders.

3. Fiordland National Park and Milford Sound

Fiordland National Park, a remote and rugged wilderness on New Zealand's South Island, is a realm where nature's grandeur is on full display. Spanning over 12,500 square kilometers, this UNESCO World Heritage site is home to a myriad of fjords, lush rainforests, and towering mountain ranges. At the heart of Fiordland lies Milford Sound, often described as the "eighth wonder of the world," an epitome of the park's breathtaking beauty.

The journey to Milford Sound is an adventure in itself, with the Milford Road weaving through some of the most stunning landscapes in the region. This scenic drive, which starts in the town of Te Anau, offers travelers glimpses of Fiordland's diverse ecosystems. As you traverse this route, the scenery shifts from rolling farmlands to dense beech forests, with dramatic mountain vistas unfolding at every turn. The Homer Tunnel, a marvel of engineering carved through sheer rock faces, marks the transition into the heart of the fjord.

Upon reaching Milford Sound, the first sight of Mitre Peak rising sharply from the water is awe-inspiring. This iconic mountain, standing at 1,692 meters, dominates the skyline and sets the stage for the fjord's dramatic landscape. The deep waters of Milford Sound are flanked by sheer cliffs and cascading waterfalls, with rain or shine adding its own unique charm to the scene. Frequent rain showers feed the waterfalls, creating a mystical atmosphere, while sunlight reveals the fjord's intricate details and mirror-like reflections.

Exploring Milford Sound by boat is an essential experience, providing a perspective that captures the fjord's scale and majesty. Cruises navigate the length of the fjord, offering close encounters with its natural wonders. Seals bask lazily on the rocks, while playful dolphins often accompany the boats, riding the bow waves with graceful agility. The chance to see rare Fiordland crested penguins, particularly during breeding season, adds to the allure of the journey.

Kayaking is another way to immerse yourself in the beauty of Milford Sound, offering a more intimate and tranquil exploration. Gliding silently through the water, kayakers can navigate closer to the waterfalls and cliffs, experiencing the fjord's serenity and the sounds of nature undisturbed. Guided kayaking tours provide safety and expertise, ensuring that even beginners can enjoy this unique perspective.

Fiordland's landscapes are not confined to the water; the park's trails offer some of New Zealand's most rewarding hiking experiences. The Milford Track, renowned as one of the world's greatest walks, spans 53 kilometers from Lake Te Anau to Sandfly Point in Milford Sound. This multi-day trek takes hikers through lush rainforests, past thundering waterfalls, and over alpine passes, culminating in a view of the fjord that is both a culmination and a celebration of the journey.

For those with limited time, shorter walks such as the Key Summit Track offer stunning vistas of the surrounding mountains and valleys. This walk, part of the Routeburn Track, ascends through beech forest to an alpine environment, providing panoramic views that encapsulate the essence of Fiordland's diverse environments.

The flora and fauna encountered along these trails are a testament to the park's ecological richness, with moss-draped trees, blooming alpine flowers, and the call of native birds creating a symphony of natural beauty.

Fiordland is also renowned for its unique geological formations, shaped by millions of years of glacial activity. The fjords themselves are deep, steep-walled inlets carved by ancient glaciers, a testament to the power of natural forces. The discovery of black coral in the waters of Milford Sound, usually found in much deeper seas, is another geological marvel, a result of the fjord's unique underwater environment.

Beyond Milford Sound, Fiordland National Park offers a wealth of other fjords and landscapes to explore. Doubtful Sound, often referred to as the "Sound of Silence," is deeper and more remote than Milford, providing a more secluded experience. Accessible via a boat ride across Lake Manapouri and a bus journey over Wilmot Pass, Doubtful Sound is a haven for wildlife, with bottlenose dolphins, fur seals, and penguins inhabiting its tranquil waters. The sense of isolation and untouched wilderness here is profound, offering a connection to nature that is both humbling and inspiring.

Preservation of Fiordland's unique environment is a key focus, with conservation efforts aimed at protecting its fragile ecosystems. The park's status as a World Heritage site underscores its global importance, and visitors are encouraged to respect the natural environment by adhering to sustainable practices. This includes minimizing waste, staying on designated trails, and supporting local conservation initiatives, ensuring that Fiordland's beauty and biodiversity are preserved for future generations.

For those seeking a glimpse into the cultural history of Fiordland, the narratives of the Māori people offer a rich tapestry of legends and traditions. The Māori have a deep connection to the land, and their stories speak of the creation of the fjords by the legendary figure Tū Te Rakiwhānoa. These tales, passed down through generations, add a layer of cultural depth to the experience of exploring Fiordland, providing insights into the spiritual significance of the landscape.

Fiordland National Park and Milford Sound represent a pinnacle of natural beauty and adventure, a place where the majesty of the natural world is both preserved and celebrated. Whether you're cruising the fjord, trekking through rainforests, or simply standing in awe of the towering peaks, the experience is one of profound connection to the Earth and its wonders. Fiordland invites you to explore, reflect, and embrace the extraordinary, leaving you with memories that resonate long after you've returned to the outside world.

4. Wildlife Encounters in Dunedin and Otago

Dunedin, a charming coastal city on New Zealand's South Island, offers a unique blend of culture, history, and nature. One of the most captivating aspects of Dunedin and the surrounding Otago region is the opportunity to encounter an array of wildlife in their natural habitats. From the rare yellow-eyed penguins to the playful sea lions, the area's diverse ecosystems provide a haven for many species, creating a wildlife experience that is both enriching and unforgettable.

The Otago Peninsula, a short drive from the city center, is a prime location for wildlife enthusiasts. This scenic stretch of land extends into the Pacific Ocean and is home to numerous species that thrive in its coastal and marine environments. The peninsula's rugged coastline, sandy beaches, and rolling hills create an ideal setting for observing wildlife in their natural settings.

One of the most iconic residents of the Otago Peninsula is the yellow-eyed penguin, or hoiho, one of the world's rarest penguin species. These shy and solitary birds can often be seen returning to their nests in the late afternoon after a day of fishing at sea. The best way to observe these penguins without disturbing them is through guided tours that provide insights into their behavior and conservation efforts. The Penguin Place, a private conservation reserve, offers guided tours that allow visitors to view penguins from specially constructed hides, ensuring minimal impact on the birds' natural environment.

Another highlight of the Otago Peninsula is the Royal Albatross Centre at Taiaroa Head, the only mainland breeding colony of the northern royal albatross. These magnificent birds, with wingspans reaching up to three meters, are a sight to behold as they glide effortlessly over the ocean. The center offers guided tours that provide an opportunity to learn about the life cycle and conservation of these majestic seabirds. The sight of an albatross returning to its nest, soaring gracefully through the sky, is a moment of awe and wonder.

The peninsula is also home to a thriving population of New Zealand fur seals and sea lions. Pilots Beach, near Taiaroa Head, is a popular spot to witness these marine mammals basking on the rocks or frolicking in the surf. Observing these animals in the wild offers a glimpse into their social interactions and playful behaviors. While the seals often rest in large groups, sea lions are more solitary and territorial, a dynamic that can be fascinating to witness.

Beyond the peninsula, the Otago region boasts a variety of other wildlife experiences. The Catlins, located to the south, is a remote and rugged area renowned for its pristine landscapes and abundant wildlife. Nugget Point, a dramatic headland in the Catlins, is a prime location for spotting a range of seabirds, including gannets, shearwaters, and the rare yellow-eyed penguins. The rocky outcrops and sheltered coves also provide habitat for fur seals and sea lions, making it a haven for marine life.

The inland areas of Otago offer their own unique wildlife encounters. The region's diverse habitats, from alpine meadows to tussock grasslands, support a variety of bird species. The kea, a charismatic alpine parrot known for its intelligence and curiosity, is often seen in the mountainous areas, providing an opportunity for interaction and observation. The region is also home to the New Zealand falcon, or kārearea, a powerful bird of prey that can be spotted hunting in open country.

Conservation plays a crucial role in the preservation of Otago's wildlife, with numerous initiatives aimed at protecting habitats and species. Many of the guided tours and wildlife centers contribute to conservation efforts, offering visitors the chance to learn about and support these vital projects. By participating in eco-friendly tours and following guidelines to minimize disturbance, visitors can enjoy the natural beauty of the region while contributing to the protection of its unique ecosystems.

In addition to the wildlife, Dunedin itself offers a rich tapestry of cultural and historical experiences. The city's Scottish heritage is reflected in its architecture, with landmarks such as the Dunedin Railway Station and Larnach Castle showcasing intricate designs and craftsmanship. The Otago Museum provides a comprehensive overview of the region's natural and cultural history, with exhibits that highlight both the indigenous Māori culture and the European settlers who shaped the city's identity.

Dunedin's commitment to preserving its natural and cultural heritage is evident in its many parks and reserves. The Dunedin Botanic Garden, the oldest in New Zealand, offers a tranquil retreat with its diverse plant collections and beautifully landscaped grounds. The garden's aviary, home to a variety of native and exotic birds, provides another opportunity for wildlife observation in a serene setting.

The vibrant arts scene in Dunedin adds another layer of depth to the city's appeal. The city's galleries, theaters, and music venues showcase local talent and international acts, creating a dynamic cultural landscape. The annual Dunedin Fringe Festival and the Dunedin Writers & Readers Festival are just a few of the events that celebrate the city's creative spirit.

Dining in Dunedin offers a taste of the region's culinary diversity, with a focus on fresh, locally sourced ingredients. The city's cafes and restaurants serve a range of cuisines, from traditional New Zealand fare to international dishes, providing a culinary journey that complements the wildlife and cultural experiences.

As you explore Dunedin and Otago, the connection between the land, its wildlife, and its people becomes increasingly evident. The opportunity to encounter rare and unique species in their natural habitats, combined with the rich cultural tapestry of the region, creates an experience that is both enlightening and inspiring. Whether you're observing the majestic albatross, exploring the rugged beauty of the Catlins, or delving into the vibrant culture of Dunedin, the memories forged in this remarkable corner of New Zealand are sure to leave a lasting impression.

5. Vineyard Tours in Marlborough

Nestled at the tip of New Zealand's South Island, the Marlborough region is synonymous with viticulture excellence, boasting a reputation for producing some of the world's finest wines. Its expansive vineyards, set against a backdrop of striking landscapes, offer a sensory journey through the art and science of winemaking. With a climate that mirrors the Mediterranean and soils that nurture diverse grape varieties, Marlborough has become a premier destination for wine enthusiasts and curious travelers alike.

Marlborough's viticultural fame is largely attributed to its Sauvignon Blanc, a varietal that has garnered international acclaim for its vibrant flavors and aromatic intensity. The region's unique terroir, characterized by long sunshine hours, cool nights, and free-draining alluvial soils, imparts distinct qualities to the grapes, resulting in wines that are crisp, zesty, and bursting with tropical fruit notes. This distinctive style has set the benchmark for Sauvignon Blanc globally, making a Marlborough wine tour a must for any aficionado.

The journey through Marlborough's vineyards begins in the town of Blenheim, the heart of the wine country. Here, an array of wineries, ranging from boutique family-owned estates to well-known international brands, open their cellar doors to visitors, offering an immersive experience into the world of winemaking. Each winery has its own story, philosophy, and approach, providing a diverse tapestry of flavors and techniques to explore.

One of the most engaging aspects of a vineyard tour is the opportunity to meet the winemakers themselves. These passionate individuals share their insights into the winemaking process, from the cultivation of the vines to the art of blending and aging. Their stories of dedication and innovation reveal the intricate balance between tradition and modernity that defines the Marlborough wine scene. Tasting sessions, often accompanied by expertly paired local cheeses and charcuterie, allow visitors to savor the nuances of each wine, guided by the expertise of those who crafted them.

Beyond Sauvignon Blanc, Marlborough's vineyards are home to a variety of other grape types that thrive in its diverse sub-regions. Chardonnay, with its elegant structure and subtle complexity, offers a refined counterpoint to the boldness of Sauvignon Blanc. Pinot Noir, cultivated in the cooler southern valleys, is celebrated for its delicate aromas and silky texture, reflecting the region's terroir with finesse. Additionally, aromatic varieties such as Riesling, Pinot Gris, and Gewürztraminer add to the region's rich tapestry of flavors, each expressing unique characteristics shaped by Marlborough's climate and soils.

The picturesque landscapes of Marlborough provide a stunning backdrop for vineyard tours, enhancing the sensory experience of wine tasting with visual splendor. The Wairau Valley, with its expansive plains and braided rivers, is home to some of the largest and most renowned vineyards in the region. The rolling hills and sheltered valleys of the Awatere Valley offer a more intimate setting, where smaller vineyards produce distinctive wines with a focus on quality and character. The Southern Valleys, with their diverse microclimates and soil profiles, add further complexity to the region's wine offerings.

Exploring Marlborough's vineyards is not only about tasting wine but also about understanding the sustainable practices that underpin the region's viticulture. Many wineries are committed to organic and biodynamic farming, reflecting a broader ethos of environmental stewardship and respect for the land. These practices not only enhance the quality and authenticity of the wines but also contribute to the preservation of Marlborough's natural beauty for future generations. Visitors are often invited to tour the vineyards, learning about the ecological principles that guide sustainable viticulture, from soil health and biodiversity to water management and energy efficiency.

For those seeking a more personalized experience, private tours and bespoke itineraries offer the opportunity to delve deeper into Marlborough's wine culture. These tailored experiences can include exclusive tastings of limited-release wines, guided tours of vineyards and cellars, and intimate lunches or dinners with winemakers. Whether traveling by car, bike, or even helicopter, these customized tours provide a deeper connection to the region and its people, creating lasting memories and a greater appreciation for the craft of winemaking.

Marlborough's culinary scene complements its wine offerings, with a focus on fresh, locally sourced ingredients that highlight the region's abundance. Many wineries feature on-site restaurants or cafes, where chefs create dishes that harmonize with the wines, showcasing the best of Marlborough's produce. From succulent seafood and grass-fed meats to seasonal fruits and vegetables, the region's cuisine is a testament to the bounty and diversity of its land and waters.

The annual Marlborough Wine and Food Festival, held in February, is a celebration of the region's viticultural and culinary achievements. This lively event brings together winemakers, chefs, and artisans from across Marlborough and beyond, offering attendees the chance to sample a wide array of wines and gourmet foods while enjoying live music and entertainment. It's a vibrant showcase of the region's creativity and passion, drawing visitors from around the world to experience the best of Marlborough in a festive atmosphere.

Throughout the year, the region's warm hospitality and welcoming spirit ensure that visitors to Marlborough's vineyards feel like part of the community. Whether you're a seasoned oenophile or a curious newcomer, the connection between the land, the wine, and the people creates an experience that is both educational and enriching. The stories of Marlborough's winemakers, the beauty of its landscapes, and the flavors of its wines come together to form a tapestry of discovery and enjoyment that lingers long after the last glass is savored.

6. The West Coast's Natural Wonders

The West Coast of New Zealand's South Island is a region of raw, untamed beauty, where the forces of nature have sculpted a landscape both dramatic and diverse. Stretching over 600 kilometers, this narrow strip of land is flanked by the Tasman Sea to the west and the imposing Southern Alps to the east. The West Coast's natural wonders are as varied as they are captivating, offering a journey through lush rainforests, towering glaciers, and rugged coastlines.

One of the most iconic features of the West Coast is its glaciers, most notably the Franz Josef and Fox Glaciers. These rivers of ice descend from the Southern Alps, reaching down into temperate rainforest, a rare phenomenon in the world of glaciology. Franz Josef Glacier, known as Kā Roimata o Hine Hukatere in Māori, is a spectacle of crevasses and seracs. Guided glacier walks provide an opportunity to explore this icy realm, with experienced guides leading the way through the frozen landscape. For those seeking an aerial perspective, helicopter tours offer breathtaking views of the glaciers' expanse, revealing the intricate patterns carved by the ice.

The nearby Fox Glacier, or Te Moeka o Tuawe, offers a similarly awe-inspiring experience. The surrounding rainforest creates a stark contrast to the glacier's icy surface, underscoring the diverse ecosystems that coexist in this region. Guided tours allow visitors to safely navigate the glacier's terrain, providing insights into its formation and the ongoing impact of climate change. The experience of standing on a glacier, surrounded by the grandeur of the Southern Alps, is one of profound connection to the natural world.

Beyond the glaciers, the West Coast is home to a wealth of other natural wonders. The Pancake Rocks and Blowholes at Punakaiki are a geological marvel, where layers of limestone have been eroded by the sea into striking formations resembling stacks of pancakes. During high tide, seawater is forced through vertical blowholes, creating dramatic spouts of water that captivate visitors. The surrounding Paparoa National Park, with its rugged cliffs and lush forests, offers a network of walking tracks that showcase the region's unique flora and fauna.

The West Coast's rainforests are a verdant tapestry of life, harboring a rich diversity of plant and animal species. The lush canopy is dominated by ancient trees, such as rimu and kahikatea, draped with epiphytes and ferns. The forest floor is a carpet of moss and leaf litter, providing habitat for native birds like the inquisitive weka and the melodious tui. Walks through these forests reveal the intricate relationships that sustain this ecosystem, offering moments of tranquility and discovery.

The region's coastline is equally captivating, with rugged cliffs, windswept beaches, and secluded coves. The Great Coast Road, a scenic drive between Westport and Greymouth, offers stunning views of the Tasman Sea and the dramatic coastal landscape. Cape Foulwind, with its lighthouse and fur seal colony, is a highlight of the route, providing a chance to observe these playful marine mammals in their natural habitat. The seals, often seen basking on the rocks or frolicking in the surf, are a reminder of the vibrant marine life that thrives along the West Coast.

The West Coast's rivers and lakes add another dimension to its natural beauty. The Buller River, one of New Zealand's longest rivers, winds its way through the region, offering opportunities for white-water rafting and jet boating. Lake Matheson, near Fox Glacier, is renowned for its mirror-like reflections of Aoraki/Mount Cook and Mount Tasman. A walking track around the lake provides vantage points to capture this stunning vista, particularly at dawn or dusk when the light creates a magical scene.

The region's geological history is evident in its many caves and karst landscapes. The Oparara Basin, with its limestone arches and honeycomb caves, is a hidden gem in the Kahurangi National Park. Guided tours of the Honeycomb Hill Caves reveal intricate stalactites and stalagmites, as well as the fossilized remains of ancient animals. The arches, formed by the erosion of limestone over millions of years, are a testament to the power of natural forces and offer a unique perspective on the region's geological past.

The West Coast's natural wonders are not limited to its landforms; its ecosystems support a range of wildlife, both on land and in the sea. The region's wetlands and estuaries are important habitats for bird species, including the rare and endangered kotuku, or white heron. The Okarito Lagoon, New Zealand's largest unmodified wetland, is a haven for birdwatchers, offering sightings of the kotuku and other wading birds. Kayaking tours provide a peaceful way to explore the lagoon's waterways, bringing you closer to this delicate ecosystem and its inhabitants.

The cultural heritage of the West Coast is woven into its natural landscape, with the Māori people holding a deep connection to the land and its stories. The West Coast is rich in pounamu, or greenstone, which has been treasured by Māori for centuries. This precious stone is found in the rivers and mountains of the region and is used to create intricate carvings and jewelry. Visitors can learn about the significance of pounamu and its role in Māori culture through guided tours and workshops, gaining an appreciation for the cultural dimensions of this natural wonder.

The West Coast's natural wonders are a testament to the beauty and power of the natural world, offering a journey through landscapes that are both ancient and dynamic. From the icy expanses of the glaciers to the lush rainforests and rugged coastlines, the region is a mosaic of ecosystems that invite exploration and reflection. Whether you're trekking on a glacier, marveling at the Pancake Rocks, or listening to the birdsong in a tranquil forest, the West Coast offers an experience that is both humbling and inspiring, leaving an indelible mark on all who venture into its wild embrace.

CHAPTER 6: KIWI HOSPITALITY AND LOCAL LIFE

1. Understanding Kiwi Culture

New Zealand's kiwi culture is a vibrant tapestry woven from the threads of its indigenous Māori heritage and European colonial influences. As you step into the world of kiwi culture, you'll find a society that values community, innovation, and a deep connection to the land. Understanding this culture involves delving into its customs, values, and the everyday lives of its people, offering insights that are both enlightening and enriching.

At the heart of kiwi culture is the Māori tradition, which has shaped New Zealand's identity in profound ways. The Māori, New Zealand's indigenous people, arrived on the islands over a thousand years ago, bringing with them rich traditions and a deep respect for nature. Māori culture is centered around the concept of mana, which signifies spiritual power and authority, and whānau, the extended family unit that forms the basis of Māori society. These principles influence everything from social interactions to governance, underscoring the importance of community and respect.

The Māori language, or te reo Māori, is an integral part of New Zealand's cultural fabric. Efforts to revive and promote te reo have seen it flourish in recent years, with increasing numbers of New Zealanders learning the language. Māori greetings and phrases are commonly used in daily life, reflecting a broader cultural renaissance. Visitors to New Zealand are often greeted with a warm "kia ora," a simple yet powerful expression of welcome and goodwill.

The powhiri, a traditional Māori welcome ceremony, is a cornerstone of Māori cultural practices. This ceremony, which takes place on marae (Māori meeting grounds), involves speeches, songs, and the hongi, a greeting where participants press their noses together to share breath. The powhiri is an expression of hospitality, symbolizing the coming together of people and the acknowledgment of shared humanity. Participating in a powhiri offers a profound introduction to the values and traditions that underpin Māori culture.

The Māori tradition of storytelling, or kōrero pūrākau, is another vital aspect of kiwi culture. Through myths and legends, Māori pass down ancestral knowledge and values, connecting generations and preserving their rich heritage. These stories often feature atua (gods) and tūpuna (ancestors), whose deeds and adventures explain the natural world and human behavior. The tale of Māui, a legendary hero who fished up the North Island, is one such story that illustrates the ingenuity and courage celebrated in Māori culture.

New Zealand's colonial history has also significantly influenced kiwi culture, with European settlers bringing their own customs and traditions. This blend has resulted in a unique cultural identity characterized by a strong sense of egalitarianism and a "can-do" attitude. Kiwis, as New Zealanders are colloquially known, pride themselves on their resourcefulness and innovation, often referred to as "kiwi ingenuity." This mindset is reflected in the country's achievements in fields such as science, sports, and the arts, where creativity and perseverance are highly valued.

Rugby holds a special place in kiwi culture, serving as both a national pastime and a source of national pride. The All Blacks, New Zealand's national rugby team, are revered for their prowess on the field and their iconic haka, a traditional Māori war dance performed before matches. The haka is a powerful expression of unity and strength, embodying the spirit of the team and the country. Rugby matches, whether at the local or international level, are social events that bring communities together, reinforcing bonds and fostering a sense of belonging.

New Zealand's commitment to environmental stewardship is another defining feature of kiwi culture. The country's breathtaking landscapes, from pristine beaches to towering mountains, are cherished by its people, who recognize the importance of preserving these natural treasures for future generations. This respect for the environment is reflected in New Zealand's commitment to sustainability and conservation, with initiatives aimed at protecting native species and reducing carbon footprints. The Māori concept of kaitiakitanga, or guardianship, embodies this ethos, emphasizing the responsibility to care for the land and its resources.

Kiwi culture is also characterized by a relaxed and informal lifestyle, where work-life balance is highly valued. The pace of life is generally laid-back, with an emphasis on enjoying the outdoors and spending time with family and friends. Social gatherings often revolve around barbecues, or "kiwi BBQs," where people come together to share food and laughter, reinforcing the importance of community and connection.

Food plays a significant role in kiwi culture, with local cuisine reflecting the country's diverse influences and abundant natural resources. Seafood, or kaimoana, is a staple, with dishes featuring fresh fish, shellfish, and the delicacy of whitebait. The hangi, a traditional Māori feast cooked in an earth oven, is a communal experience that brings people together to celebrate and share. New Zealand's burgeoning wine industry, particularly its world-renowned Sauvignon Blanc, adds another dimension to the culinary landscape, offering flavors that complement the country's fresh and vibrant dishes.

The arts are a vibrant expression of kiwi culture, with New Zealand's creative scene thriving across various disciplines. From traditional Māori carving and weaving to contemporary visual arts, music, and theater, the country's artistic output reflects its rich cultural heritage and innovative spirit. Festivals and events celebrating the arts, such as the New Zealand Festival and the Māori Arts Festival, provide platforms for artists to showcase their work and engage with audiences, fostering a dynamic and inclusive cultural environment.

Understanding kiwi culture is a journey into the heart of a nation that values diversity, creativity, and connection. It is a culture that embraces its roots while continually evolving, shaped by the people and landscapes that define New Zealand. Whether you're participating in a powhiri, cheering on the All Blacks, or exploring the country's natural wonders, the warmth and hospitality of kiwi culture are sure to leave a lasting impression. It's a culture that invites you to engage, learn, and appreciate the unique blend of traditions and innovations that make New Zealand a truly special place.

2. Staying in Local Homesteads

Staying in local homesteads offers travelers an enriching opportunity to experience a destination through the eyes of its residents, providing a deeper understanding of the local culture and lifestyle. In New Zealand, where the natural beauty and diverse landscapes are matched by the warmth and hospitality of its people, staying in a homestead is a chance to connect with the country's unique identity in an intimate and meaningful way.

Homesteads in New Zealand are often situated in rural areas, surrounded by breathtaking scenery that ranges from rolling farmlands to lush forests and rugged coastlines. These accommodations are typically family-run, offering guests a personalized experience that larger hotels or resorts cannot match.

The hosts, often lifelong residents of the area, are eager to share their knowledge and stories, providing insights into the local history, traditions, and way of life.

The charm of staying in a homestead lies in the authenticity of the experience. Unlike more commercial accommodations, homesteads offer a glimpse into the daily rhythms and routines of local life. Guests can expect to enjoy hearty home-cooked meals, often prepared with ingredients sourced from the property's gardens or nearby farms. These meals are a celebration of local flavors and culinary traditions, from the classic roast lamb to freshly caught seafood and seasonal vegetables. Breakfast might include homemade preserves and freshly baked bread, while dinners are a communal affair, where stories are exchanged and friendships forged over a shared table.

One of the highlights of staying in a homestead is the opportunity to participate in everyday activities and learn new skills. Depending on the location and focus of the homestead, guests might find themselves helping with farm chores, such as feeding animals or collecting eggs, or learning traditional crafts like weaving or pottery. These hands-on experiences provide a deeper appreciation for the hard work and dedication required to maintain a rural lifestyle, as well as the satisfaction that comes from living in harmony with the land.

For those interested in exploring the great outdoors, homesteads often serve as an ideal base for adventures in the surrounding countryside. Hosts, with their extensive local knowledge, can recommend the best hiking trails, fishing spots, or scenic drives, ensuring that guests experience the hidden gems of the region. Some homesteads even offer guided tours or activities, such as horseback riding or kayaking, allowing guests to explore the landscape with the benefit of local expertise.

In addition to the natural beauty and recreational opportunities, staying in a homestead provides a chance to engage with the local community. Many homesteads are located within small towns or villages, where guests can visit local markets, artisan shops, or cultural events. These interactions offer a window into the community's unique character and traditions, fostering a sense of connection and understanding between visitors and residents.

A key aspect of the homestead experience is the opportunity to learn about and support sustainable and eco-friendly practices. Many homesteads in New Zealand are committed to preserving the environment and promoting sustainable living, incorporating practices such as organic gardening, water conservation, and renewable energy use. By staying in a homestead, guests can witness these practices firsthand and gain inspiration for incorporating similar principles into their own lives.

For families traveling with children, homesteads offer a safe and welcoming environment where young ones can learn and explore. The open spaces and natural surroundings provide ample opportunities for outdoor play and adventure, while the close-knit family atmosphere fosters a sense of security and belonging. Children can also benefit from the educational aspects of the homestead experience, learning about agriculture, wildlife, and the importance of environmental stewardship in a hands-on and engaging way.

Choosing to stay in a local homestead is not only a way to immerse oneself in the local culture and lifestyle, but also a way to make a positive impact on the community. By supporting family-run businesses, travelers contribute to the local economy and help preserve the traditions and way of life that make these communities unique. Many homesteads also partner with local artisans and producers, offering guests the chance to purchase handmade goods and locally sourced products, further supporting the community and its craftspeople.

The memories forged during a stay in a homestead often linger long after the trip has ended. The warmth of the hosts, the beauty of the surroundings, and the authenticity of the experience create lasting impressions that enrich one's understanding of the destination. For many travelers, these personal connections and experiences become the highlight of their journey, offering a sense of fulfillment and belonging that transcends the typical tourist experience.

In an increasingly connected world, where travel can sometimes feel impersonal and homogenized, staying in a local homestead offers a refreshing alternative. It is a chance to slow down, step off the beaten path, and engage with a place and its people in a meaningful and respectful way. Whether it's sharing stories around the dinner table, exploring the natural wonders of the region, or learning a new skill, the homestead experience is a celebration of the simple pleasures and profound connections that make travel truly transformative.

3. New Zealand's Culinary Delights

New Zealand's culinary landscape is a rich mosaic that reflects its diverse cultural heritage and bountiful natural resources. This island nation, renowned for its pristine environments and vibrant ecosystems, offers a gastronomic journey that is as varied and dynamic as its landscapes. From traditional Māori hangi to contemporary fusion cuisine, New Zealand's culinary delights provide a tantalizing exploration of flavors and techniques that captivate both locals and visitors.

Central to New Zealand's culinary identity is its emphasis on fresh, locally sourced ingredients. The country's temperate climate and fertile soils yield an abundance of produce, from succulent fruits and vegetables to premium meats and seafood. This farm-to-table ethos is embraced by chefs and home cooks alike, who celebrate the natural flavors of the land and sea by allowing the ingredients to shine in their dishes.

Seafood is a cornerstone of New Zealand cuisine, with the country's extensive coastline offering a wealth of maritime treasures. The waters around New Zealand are home to a diverse array of seafood, including green-lipped mussels, crayfish, paua (abalone), and snapper. These delicacies are often prepared simply, grilled or steamed to preserve their natural flavors, and served with a squeeze of lemon or a dash of local olive oil. For a truly authentic experience, visitors can enjoy freshly shucked oysters at a coastal eatery or sample whitebait fritters, a beloved Kiwi dish made with tiny, delicate fish.

Lamb is another iconic component of New Zealand's culinary repertoire, reflecting the country's rich pastoral heritage. New Zealand lamb is celebrated for its tenderness and flavor, a result of the sheep grazing on lush, green pastures. Whether roasted to perfection and served with seasonal vegetables or slow-cooked in a hearty stew, lamb dishes are a quintessential part of the Kiwi dining experience. Many restaurants and eateries offer innovative takes on lamb, incorporating international spices and techniques to create dishes that are both comforting and contemporary.

The Māori influence on New Zealand cuisine is both profound and enduring, with traditional cooking methods and ingredients continuing to inspire modern culinary practices. The hangi, a traditional Maori method of cooking food in an earth oven, is a communal feast that embodies the spirit of togetherness and sharing. Meats, vegetables, and kumara (sweet potatoes) are wrapped in leaves and placed over hot stones in a pit, where they are slow-cooked to tender perfection. The smoky, earthy flavors of a hangi are a testament to the deep connection between the Māori people and the land, offering a unique and memorable dining experience.

New Zealand's burgeoning wine industry adds another dimension to its culinary landscape, with the country's vineyards producing world-class wines that complement its diverse cuisine. Marlborough, renowned for its Sauvignon Blanc, is a highlight of New Zealand's wine regions, with its vibrant, aromatic wines pairing beautifully with seafood and lighter dishes. The Central Otago region is celebrated for its Pinot Noir, a wine that harmonizes with the rich flavors of lamb and game meats. Wine tours and tastings provide an opportunity to explore the nuances of New Zealand's varietals, guided by the expertise of local vintners who share their passion for the craft.

The country's multicultural society has also left its mark on its culinary scene, resulting in a fusion of flavors that reflects New Zealand's global connections. Asian influences are particularly prominent, with dishes incorporating ingredients and techniques from Japan, Thailand, and China. Sushi is a popular choice, often featuring locally caught fish and innovative flavor combinations. Vietnamese pho and Thai curries have also found a place in the Kiwi culinary repertoire, offering fragrant and spicy options that appeal to diverse palates.

New Zealand's commitment to sustainability and ethical practices is evident in its culinary industry, with many chefs and producers prioritizing organic and environmentally friendly methods. Farmers' markets and artisanal food festivals are a testament to this ethos, showcasing the best of local produce and products. These markets offer a chance to connect with growers and producers, learning about the journey from farm to table and discovering the stories behind the food.

For those with a sweet tooth, New Zealand offers a variety of desserts and confections that are sure to delight. Pavlova, a meringue-based dessert topped with whipped cream and fresh fruit, is a national favorite, celebrated for its light, airy texture and vibrant flavors. Hokey pokey ice cream, featuring crunchy honeycomb toffee pieces, is a quintessential Kiwi treat that captures the playful side of New Zealand's culinary creativity. Additionally, artisanal chocolate makers are gaining recognition for their handcrafted creations, using locally sourced ingredients to produce indulgent confections that are both innovative and delicious.

New Zealand's culinary delights are as much about the experience as they are about the food itself. Dining in New Zealand is often a relaxed and convivial affair, where the emphasis is on enjoying good company and savoring the moment. Whether it's a casual barbecue on the beach, a fine dining experience in a city restaurant, or a traditional hangi in a rural village, the act of sharing a meal is a celebration of connection and community.

The country's culinary landscape is constantly evolving, with chefs and home cooks alike experimenting with new flavors and techniques while honoring the rich traditions that have shaped New Zealand's food culture. This dynamic interplay between innovation and tradition ensures that there is always something new and exciting to discover, whether you're a first-time visitor or a lifelong resident.

In conclusion, New Zealand's culinary delights offer a sensory journey through a land of abundance and diversity. From the freshest seafood and finest meats to innovative fusion dishes and traditional Māori fare, the country's cuisine is a reflection of its people, its landscapes, and its values. It invites you to taste, explore, and connect, creating memories that linger long after the meal is over.

4. Festivals and Events Throughout the Year

New Zealand's vibrant tapestry of festivals and events reflects its rich cultural diversity, lively arts scene, and deep connection to its natural environment. Throughout the year, these celebrations offer glimpses into the country's soul, inviting both locals and visitors to partake in the joyous spirit that defines Kiwi life. Each event, whether steeped in tradition or pulsating with modern flair, provides an opportunity to connect, learn, and revel in the unique culture of Aotearoa.

One of the most significant celebrations is Waitangi Day, observed on February 6th. It commemorates the signing of the Treaty of Waitangi in 1840, a foundational document in New Zealand's history. This day is marked by ceremonies and events held at Waitangi in the Bay of Islands, where the treaty was signed. These gatherings offer a chance to reflect on the relationship between Māori and Pākehā (non-Māori New Zealanders), featuring cultural performances, speeches, and traditional Māori ceremonies. For those visiting the country, attending Waitangi Day celebrations provides a profound insight into New Zealand's bicultural heritage and ongoing journey towards reconciliation and unity.

As summer unfolds, the country comes alive with music festivals that draw crowds from all corners. Rhythm and Vines, held in Gisborne over New Year's, is one of the premier music festivals, renowned for its diverse lineup of international and local artists. Set against the backdrop of stunning vineyards and beaches, the festival is a celebration of music, nature, and the vibrant energy of summer. Other notable music festivals include Laneway Festival in Auckland and WOMAD in New Plymouth, which showcase a range of genres and cultural influences, from indie and electronic to world music and traditional sounds.

The arts are celebrated with fervor in New Zealand, and the New Zealand Festival of the Arts, held biennially in Wellington, is a testament to the country's creative spirit. This multi-disciplinary festival features a captivating array of performances, including theater, dance, music, and visual arts. Artists from around the globe converge in the capital city to present works that challenge, inspire, and entertain. The festival serves as a platform for cultural exchange and artistic innovation, fostering a dynamic dialogue between artists and audiences.

For film enthusiasts, the New Zealand International Film Festival is a highlight of the cultural calendar. Held annually in major cities across the country, the festival showcases a diverse selection of films, from cutting-edge independent productions to acclaimed international releases. It offers a window into the world of cinema, where storytelling transcends boundaries and sparks conversations. The festival is an opportunity to experience the magic of film in iconic venues, from historic theaters to contemporary cinemas, each screening a journey into the art of filmmaking.

Autumn in New Zealand brings with it the Hokitika Wildfoods Festival, a unique culinary event that captures the adventurous spirit of the West Coast. This one-of-a-kind festival challenges attendees to expand their palates with a range of exotic and unusual delicacies, from huhu grubs and wild game to traditional Māori fare. The festival celebrates the region's rugged landscape and resourcefulness, offering live entertainment, cooking demonstrations, and a vibrant atmosphere that is both daring and delightful.

As the year progresses, the Matariki Festival heralds the Māori New Year, a time for reflection, renewal, and celebration. Matariki, the Māori name for the Pleiades star cluster, rises in the winter sky, marking the start of the new year in the Māori lunar calendar. Communities across New Zealand gather to honor this occasion with cultural performances, storytelling, and feasting. Matariki is a time to remember the past, celebrate the present, and prepare for the future, emphasizing themes of unity, gratitude, and growth. Participating in Matariki events offers a deep connection to Māori traditions and a sense of belonging to the rhythms of the natural world.

Springtime in New Zealand is adorned with the colors and fragrances of the Tulip Festival in Hamilton. This floral extravaganza is a celebration of the vibrant beauty of Tulips, with displays that transform Hamilton Gardens into a kaleidoscope of color. The festival features garden tours, workshops, and live music, drawing visitors into a world of horticultural wonder. The Tulip Festival is a testament to the transformative power of nature, inviting attendees to revel in the beauty of spring and the joy of new beginnings.

The festive season in New Zealand is marked by Christmas parades and Santa festivals, bringing communities together in a spirit of joy and generosity. These events, held in towns and cities across the country, feature colorful floats, marching bands, and, of course, Santa Claus himself. The parades are a highlight for families, offering a chance to create cherished memories and celebrate the holiday season with loved ones.

In addition to these major events, New Zealand hosts a myriad of local and regional festivals that showcase the diverse passions and talents of its communities. From food and wine festivals in Marlborough and Hawke's Bay to arts and culture celebrations in small towns and cities, these events highlight the unique character of each region, offering visitors an opportunity to delve deeper into the local way of life.

Attending festivals and events in New Zealand is not just about witnessing cultural performances or sampling local delicacies; it's about becoming part of a collective experience that transcends the ordinary. These gatherings are a celebration of life, inviting participants to connect with each other and the world around them in meaningful ways. Whether you're dancing under the stars at a music festival, savoring the flavors of a wild foods event, or reflecting on the past and future during Matariki, you'll find that New Zealand's festivals offer a rich tapestry of experiences that enrich the soul and ignite the imagination.

In the vibrant rhythm of these events, the essence of New Zealand comes alive, offering a journey that is as exhilarating as it is enlightening. The festivals and events throughout the year are an invitation to explore the heart of Kiwi culture, where the spirit of community and creativity thrives in every celebration.

5. Shopping for Local Art and Souvenirs

Exploring the art and souvenirs of a destination offers a unique insight into its cultural identity and history. In New Zealand, shopping for local art and souvenirs is a journey into the heart of its creative spirit, where traditional Māori craftsmanship meets contemporary artistic expression. From bustling urban galleries to quaint rural craft shops, the options are as diverse as the landscapes that inspire them, offering treasures that serve as meaningful mementos of your visit.

The Māori culture, which forms the cornerstone of New Zealand's identity, is celebrated through a range of traditional crafts that make for captivating souvenirs. Carved wood items, known as whakairo, are particularly popular, each piece telling a story through intricate patterns and symbols. These carvings, whether adorning a small pendant or a larger sculpture, are imbued with spiritual significance, making them a cherished keepsake. Bone and greenstone (pounamu) carvings are also highly sought after, with each design carrying its own meaning, from protection to strength. When purchasing these items, it's important to understand their cultural significance and support artisans who are respectful of traditional methods and meanings.

Textiles are another avenue through which Māori culture is expressed, with weaving being a traditional art form that has been passed down through generations. Kete, woven flax baskets, are both practical and beautiful, featuring patterns that reflect the weaver's whakapapa (ancestry). These baskets, along with other woven items like cloaks and wall hangings, make for unique and culturally significant souvenirs that capture the essence of Māori artistry.

In addition to traditional crafts, New Zealand's contemporary art scene offers a wealth of options for those seeking unique and original pieces. Artists across the country draw inspiration from the stunning natural environment and the cultural tapestry of New Zealand, producing works that range from abstract paintings and sculptures to photography and digital art. Galleries in major cities like Auckland and Wellington showcase both emerging and established artists, providing a platform for diverse voices and perspectives. Acquiring a piece of contemporary art not only supports the local creative community but also brings a piece of New Zealand's vibrant art scene into your home.

For those with a penchant for wearable art, New Zealand's fashion and jewelry designers offer an array of distinctive creations that blend traditional influences with modern aesthetics. Designers often incorporate local materials, such as paua shell, into their pieces, capturing the colors and textures of the natural landscape. Whether it's a handcrafted silver ring or a bespoke garment, these items make for memorable souvenirs that reflect the innovative spirit of New Zealand's design community.

No shopping experience in New Zealand would be complete without exploring its artisanal food and beverage offerings. Local markets and specialty stores are brimming with culinary delights that make for delicious souvenirs. Manuka honey, known for its unique flavor and health benefits, is a quintessential Kiwi product that can be found in a variety of forms, from jars of pure honey to infused chocolates and skincare products. New Zealand wines, particularly those from regions like Marlborough and Central Otago, are also a popular choice, offering a taste of the country's renowned viticulture.

Craft beer enthusiasts will find much to delight in, as New Zealand's thriving craft beer scene boasts a wide range of innovative brews that capture the adventurous palate of Kiwi brewers. Many breweries offer tasting packs or specially curated selections, making it easy to bring a taste of New Zealand's craft beer culture home. Similarly, locally roasted coffee and handcrafted chocolates are perfect for those seeking a more indulgent souvenir.

When shopping for souvenirs, it's essential to consider the impact of your purchases on the local community and environment. Opting for items that are sustainably produced and ethically sourced supports artisans and businesses that prioritize ecological and social responsibility. Many New Zealand artists and producers are committed to environmentally friendly practices, using renewable materials and reducing waste in their processes. By choosing such products, you contribute to the preservation of New Zealand's natural beauty and cultural heritage.

Exploring local markets and craft fairs is an excellent way to immerse yourself in the vibrant atmosphere of New Zealand's creative community. These events offer the chance to meet the artists and craftspeople behind the products, gaining insight into their inspirations and techniques. Markets like the Wellington Night Market and the Christchurch Arts Centre Market showcase a diverse array of goods, from handcrafted jewelry and textiles to gourmet foods and homewares. These markets are not only a feast for the senses but also a celebration of the creativity and diversity that define New Zealand culture.

In addition to physical items, experiences themselves can serve as meaningful souvenirs, capturing the essence of your time in New Zealand. Workshops and classes, such as pottery or traditional carving, allow you to engage with local crafts in a hands-on way, creating your own piece of art to take home. These experiences provide a deeper understanding of the skills and traditions involved, offering a personal connection to the culture and a tangible reminder of your journey.

As you explore the art and souvenirs of New Zealand, you'll find that each piece tells a story—a reflection of the land, its people, and their creative spirit. Whether it's a traditional Māori carving, a piece of contemporary art, or a taste of the country's culinary delights, these items serve as a bridge between your experiences and the memories you'll carry with you. They are reminders of the beauty and diversity of New Zealand, inviting you to recall the moments of discovery and connection that made your visit truly special.

CHAPTER 7: PLANNING YOUR ADVENTURE

1. Creating Your Itinerary

Crafting an itinerary for an adventure in New Zealand is akin to painting on a vast canvas filled with vibrant possibilities. The country's diverse landscapes, rich cultural heritage, and myriad activities offer endless opportunities for exploration and discovery. To make the most of your journey, a well-thought-out itinerary is essential, balancing spontaneity with structured planning to ensure both relaxation and excitement.

Begin by determining the duration of your trip, which will serve as the foundation for your itinerary. Whether you have a week or a month, New Zealand's compact size allows for a variety of experiences without the need for extensive travel time. However, it's important to focus on quality over quantity, allowing enough time in each location to fully appreciate its unique offerings.

Once you've established the length of your stay, consider the regions you wish to explore. The North Island and South Island each boast distinct landscapes and attractions. The North Island is renowned for its geothermal wonders, Māori culture, and bustling cities like Auckland and Wellington. In contrast, the South Island offers dramatic mountain ranges, fjords, and pristine lakes, with highlights including Queenstown, the adventure capital, and the serene Marlborough wine region. Researching each region's attractions will help you prioritize the experiences that align with your interests, whether they be outdoor adventures, cultural immersion, or culinary delights.

Next, outline the key destinations you wish to visit, taking into account travel times between locations. New Zealand's well-maintained road network and domestic flight options make it easy to traverse the country, but it's crucial to factor in travel time to avoid feeling rushed. For those who prefer a slower pace, consider focusing on one island or region to explore more thoroughly. This approach allows for deeper engagement with the local environment and culture, fostering a more meaningful connection to the places you visit.

Integrating a mix of activities and experiences into your itinerary ensures a well-rounded adventure. New Zealand offers an array of outdoor pursuits, from hiking and biking to water sports and wildlife encounters. The country's renowned Great Walks, such as the Milford Track and Tongariro Alpine Crossing, provide an opportunity to immerse yourself in its breathtaking natural beauty. For thrill-seekers, adventure activities like bungee jumping, skydiving, and white-water rafting offer an adrenaline-pumping experience amid stunning scenery.

Equally important is the inclusion of cultural experiences that provide insight into New Zealand's rich heritage. Visiting a marae, a traditional Māori meeting ground, offers a glimpse into the customs and traditions of the indigenous people. Attending a cultural performance or participating in a workshop can deepen your understanding of Māori art, music, and storytelling. Additionally, exploring the country's vibrant arts scene, from galleries and museums to street art and festivals, offers a window into the creativity and diversity that define New Zealand culture.

While planning your itinerary, consider the timing of your visit and any seasonal events or festivals that may enhance your experience. New Zealand's climate varies across regions, with the summer months (December to February) offering warm weather ideal for outdoor activities. Winter (June to August) is perfect for skiing and snowboarding in the alpine regions. Spring and autumn provide milder temperatures and fewer crowds, making them ideal for those seeking a quieter experience. Keep an eye on local event calendars for festivals, markets, and cultural celebrations that may coincide with your visit, adding an extra layer of richness to your journey.

Accommodation plays a crucial role in any adventure, and New Zealand offers a wide range of options to suit different preferences and budgets. From luxury lodges and boutique hotels to charming B&Bs and budget-friendly hostels, the choices are plentiful. For a more immersive experience, consider staying in local homesteads or eco-lodges that offer a connection to the land and its people. Booking accommodations in advance, especially during peak travel seasons, ensures availability and allows for peace of mind as you embark on your adventure.

Transportation is another key consideration when planning your itinerary. Renting a car or campervan offers the freedom to explore at your own pace, with the flexibility to deviate from your planned route and discover hidden gems along the way. New Zealand's scenic driving routes, such as the Pacific Coast Highway and the Southern Scenic Route, provide breathtaking vistas and opportunities for impromptu stops. For those who prefer not to drive, public transportation options, including buses and trains, are available, as well as guided tours that offer a hassle-free way to explore popular destinations.

While structure is important, allowing room for spontaneity can lead to unexpected and rewarding experiences. Build in downtime to relax and absorb the atmosphere of each location, leaving space for serendipitous encounters and discoveries. Whether it's stumbling upon a secluded beach, joining a local gathering, or simply enjoying the tranquility of New Zealand's natural surroundings, these unplanned moments often become the highlights of a journey.

Finally, ensure your itinerary includes practical considerations such as travel insurance, visas, and health and safety preparations. Familiarize yourself with local customs and regulations, and be mindful of New Zealand's biosecurity measures, which aim to protect its unique ecosystems. Packing appropriately for the climate and activities you plan to undertake is essential, with layers and sturdy footwear recommended for outdoor adventures.

Crafting an itinerary for New Zealand is a dynamic process that requires careful consideration and flexibility. By balancing planned activities with the freedom to explore, you'll create an adventure that captures the essence of this remarkable country. Each day will unfold as a new chapter in your journey, filled with discovery, connection, and unforgettable experiences that linger long after you've returned home.

2. Transportation Options and Tips

Navigating New Zealand's diverse landscapes is an adventure in itself, and understanding the transportation options available can greatly enhance your travel experience. Whether you're traversing the rugged coastlines, exploring vibrant cities, or venturing into the serene countryside, choosing the right mode of transportation is key to a seamless journey.

Renting a car is one of the most popular ways to explore New Zealand, offering the freedom to travel at your own pace and the flexibility to discover off-the-beaten-path destinations. The country's well-maintained roads and scenic routes provide an enjoyable driving experience, with each turn revealing stunning vistas and hidden gems. When planning a road trip, consider renting a vehicle that suits the terrain and length of your journey. For those planning to explore more remote or rugged areas, a four-wheel-drive vehicle may be advantageous.

Driving in New Zealand requires a valid driver's license, and it's important to familiarize yourself with local road rules and conditions. New Zealanders drive on the left side of the road, and many rural roads are narrow and winding, requiring careful navigation. Speed limits vary depending on the area, with urban limits typically at 50 km/h and open roads at 100 km/h. Additionally, it's essential to account for weather conditions, which can change rapidly, particularly in alpine regions. Always check weather forecasts and road conditions before embarking on your journey, ensuring a safe and enjoyable trip.

For travelers who prefer not to drive, public transportation offers a convenient and cost-effective alternative. Major cities, including Auckland, Wellington, and Christchurch, boast comprehensive bus networks that provide easy access to key attractions and neighborhoods. Intercity buses connect towns and cities across the country, offering a comfortable and affordable way to explore New Zealand's diverse regions. When planning your route, consider purchasing a travel pass, which allows unlimited travel on certain bus networks and can result in significant savings.

Trains provide another scenic option for traversing New Zealand, with routes that showcase the country's breathtaking landscapes. The Northern Explorer links Auckland and Wellington, offering panoramic views of the central North Island's volcanic plateau. The TranzAlpine, regarded as one of the world's great train journeys, traverses the South Island from Christchurch to Greymouth, passing through the Southern Alps and lush rainforests. While train travel is limited compared to other transportation modes, it provides a unique perspective on New Zealand's natural beauty.

For those seeking to cover greater distances in a shorter time, domestic flights are a viable option. New Zealand's extensive network of airports connects major cities and regional hubs, making air travel a convenient choice for inter-island journeys or reaching more remote locations. Airlines such as Air New Zealand and Jetstar offer frequent flights, with competitive fares available when booked in advance. Keep in mind that smaller regional airports may have limited services, so plan accordingly and allow extra time for travel to and from the airport.

Cycling enthusiasts will find New Zealand to be a paradise for two-wheeled adventures, with dedicated cycle trails and bike-friendly cities offering endless opportunities to explore. The New Zealand Cycle Trail network, known as Nga Haerenga, features a range of trails that cater to all skill levels, from leisurely rides through vineyards to challenging mountain routes. Cycling allows for an immersive experience, connecting you with the landscape and local communities in a way that other modes of transportation cannot. When planning a cycling trip, ensure your bike is well-maintained and equipped for the terrain, and consider using a GPS or map to navigate unfamiliar routes.

For a truly unique perspective on New Zealand's landscapes, consider incorporating ferry travel into your itinerary. The Interislander and Bluebridge ferries connect the North and South Islands across the Cook Strait, offering a scenic journey with stunning views of the Marlborough Sounds and Wellington's rugged coastline. Ferries also operate between smaller islands, such as Waiheke and Stewart Island, providing access to secluded beaches, hiking trails, and wildlife reserves. Booking ferry tickets in advance is recommended, particularly during peak travel seasons, to secure your preferred departure times.

Regardless of your chosen mode of transportation, there are a few universal tips that can enhance your travel experience in New Zealand. First, consider the environmental impact of your journey and explore sustainable travel options where possible. Many transportation providers offer eco-friendly alternatives, such as hybrid rental cars and carbon-offset programs. Supporting local businesses and choosing accommodations that prioritize sustainability can also contribute to a more responsible travel experience.

Second, allow for flexibility in your itinerary, as unexpected delays or detours can lead to memorable experiences. New Zealand's diverse landscapes and vibrant communities offer countless opportunities for spontaneous exploration, so embrace the unexpected and remain open to new adventures. Whether it's discovering a hidden waterfall, stumbling upon a local market, or joining a community event, these unplanned moments often become the highlights of a trip.

Finally, prioritize safety and preparedness, particularly when venturing into remote or challenging environments. Ensure your vehicle or bicycle is well-equipped for the conditions, and carry essential supplies such as water, food, and a first aid kit. Familiarize yourself with New Zealand's safety guidelines, including outdoor safety and emergency procedures, and always inform someone of your travel plans and expected return time.

Navigating New Zealand's transportation options offers a gateway to the country's remarkable landscapes and cultural experiences. Whether you're driving along scenic coastlines, soaring above majestic mountains, or cycling through tranquil vineyards, each journey is an opportunity to connect with the essence of Aotearoa. By choosing the right transportation mode and embracing the spirit of adventure, you'll create unforgettable memories that capture the beauty and diversity of this extraordinary land.

3. Best Times to Visit Based on Activities

Choosing the best time to visit New Zealand largely depends on the activities you wish to pursue. With its diverse landscapes and varying climates, the country offers a wealth of opportunities throughout the year. From snow-capped mountains and lush rainforests to golden beaches and vibrant cities, each season brings its own unique experiences. Understanding the influence of the seasons on your chosen activities can help ensure a fulfilling and memorable journey.

For those captivated by winter sports, the months from June to August present the ideal window. The Southern Alps transform into a playground for skiing and snowboarding enthusiasts, with popular destinations like Queenstown and Wanaka offering world-class slopes and facilities. The Remarkables, Cardrona, and Treble Cone ski areas are renowned for their breathtaking views and diverse terrain catering to all skill levels. Winter is also a time for après-ski relaxation, with cozy lodges and hot pools providing a perfect retreat after a day on the slopes.

The warmer months from December to February are perfect for those seeking sun-soaked adventures. New Zealand's beaches are at their best, inviting visitors to indulge in swimming, surfing, and sunbathing. The North Island boasts stunning coastal spots such as the Bay of Islands, with its sheltered bays and marine life, and the Coromandel Peninsula, known for its golden sands and natural hot springs. The South Island's Abel Tasman National Park offers kayaking and hiking opportunities along its pristine coastline, where turquoise waters meet lush native bush.

Spring, from September to November, heralds a time of renewal and growth, making it an ideal season for exploring New Zealand's famous hiking trails. The Great Walks, including the Milford Track, Routeburn Track, and Tongariro Alpine Crossing, showcase the country's diverse ecosystems and awe-inspiring landscapes. Spring also brings an explosion of color as wildflowers bloom across the country, providing a picturesque backdrop for outdoor adventures. This time of year is less crowded, offering a more tranquil experience and the chance to connect with nature on a deeper level.

Autumn, from March to May, is a season of transformation, where vibrant foliage adds a new dimension to the landscape. This is an excellent time for wine enthusiasts to explore New Zealand's renowned wine regions, such as Marlborough and Central Otago. The grape harvest is in full swing, and wineries offer tastings and tours that provide insight into the winemaking process. The cooler temperatures and stunning autumn colors create an ideal setting for leisurely vineyard tours and sampling the country's award-winning wines.

For wildlife enthusiasts, the timing of your visit can greatly impact the likelihood of spotting New Zealand's unique fauna. Spring and early summer are prime times for birdwatching, as many species are nesting and raising their young. The Otago Peninsula is home to colonies of royal albatrosses and yellow-eyed penguins, while the forests of the North Island host the iconic kiwi bird. Marine life is abundant year-round, but the warmer months increase the chances of encountering dolphins, whales, and seals along the coast.

Fishing enthusiasts will find New Zealand's waters teeming with opportunities, with different seasons offering distinct experiences. The summer months are ideal for fly fishing in the country's pristine rivers and lakes, with trout being a popular catch. Saltwater fishing is best from December to April, when species like snapper and kingfish are plentiful. Chartering a fishing boat provides access to prime locations and the chance to learn from experienced local guides.

Cultural experiences are woven into the fabric of New Zealand's seasonal calendar, with events and festivals that reflect the country's rich heritage and contemporary creativity. The summer months are alive with music festivals, outdoor concerts, and cultural events that celebrate the arts and diversity of Kiwi life. In winter, the Matariki

Festival marks the Māori New Year, with events across the country honoring traditional practices and fostering a sense of community.

No matter the season, New Zealand's geothermal wonders are a year-round attraction, offering relaxation and rejuvenation. The North Island's Rotorua and Taupo regions are renowned for their hot springs, geysers, and mud pools, providing a natural spa experience amid stunning landscapes. Visiting these geothermal sites in cooler months offers a soothing contrast to the crisp air, making it an inviting option for travelers seeking tranquility.

Understanding the impact of the seasons on New Zealand's natural environment and activity offerings is crucial in planning a trip that aligns with your interests. Each season brings its own charm and challenges, shaping the experiences available to visitors. By aligning your travel plans with your preferred activities and the best times to enjoy them, you can create a journey that encompasses the essence of New Zealand, filled with discovery, delight, and unforgettable memories.

4. Health and Safety Considerations

When embarking on an adventure in New Zealand, prioritizing health and safety is crucial for a successful and enjoyable experience. The country's diverse landscapes, from towering mountains and dense forests to serene beaches and bustling cities, offer a wide range of activities, each with its own set of safety considerations. By being informed and prepared, travelers can minimize risks and ensure their well-being throughout their journey.

Understanding the natural environment is a fundamental aspect of staying safe in New Zealand. The country's weather can be unpredictable, particularly in mountainous regions where conditions can change rapidly. Before heading out on any outdoor activity, check the weather forecast and be prepared for sudden shifts. Dressing in layers is advisable, allowing you to adjust to changing temperatures and conditions. Rain and windproof outerwear, along with sturdy footwear, are essential for staying dry and maintaining traction on varied terrain.

New Zealand's sun is notably strong due to its geographic location and minimal air pollution. Protecting yourself from harmful UV rays is vital, even on cloudy days. Wearing a wide-brimmed hat, sunglasses, and applying a high SPF sunscreen can prevent sunburn and reduce the risk of long-term skin damage. Staying hydrated is equally important, especially during outdoor activities, as dehydration can occur quickly in sunny or windy conditions.

Outdoor enthusiasts should be aware of the specific risks associated with their chosen activities. Hikers and trekkers should familiarize themselves with the trail's difficulty level, length, and any potential hazards. Carrying a map, compass, or GPS device is recommended, along with a basic first aid kit and sufficient food and water supplies. Inform someone of your plans and expected return time, and consider using New Zealand's Mountain Safety Council resources for guidance on safe hiking practices.

Water-based activities, such as swimming, kayaking, and boating, offer unique perspectives on New Zealand's natural beauty but require careful attention to safety. Always check local conditions and advisories before entering the water, and be aware of strong currents, tides, and weather changes. Wearing a life jacket is essential for boating and kayaking, and novice participants should consider guided tours or lessons to gain confidence and skills.

New Zealand's wildlife, while generally not dangerous, includes certain species that require caution. Sandflies, particularly prevalent in the South Island's Fiordland region, can cause itchy bites.

Applying insect repellent and wearing long sleeves and pants can help minimize discomfort. In rural areas, be mindful of farm animals and adhere to posted signs and guidelines to ensure your safety and theirs.

In urban environments, general safety precautions are similar to those in other developed countries. New Zealand is considered one of the safest countries in the world, with low crime rates. However, it's always wise to remain vigilant, especially in crowded areas or unfamiliar settings. Securing your belongings, avoiding poorly lit areas at night, and being aware of your surroundings can help prevent theft or other incidents.

Health considerations should also be a priority when planning your trip. New Zealand's healthcare system is of high quality, but travelers should ensure they have adequate travel insurance that covers medical emergencies and evacuation if necessary. It's advisable to carry any necessary medications in their original packaging, accompanied by a doctor's note or prescription if required. Pharmacies in New Zealand can provide assistance with minor ailments, and emergency services are widely available.

Food and water safety is generally not a concern in New Zealand, as the country's tap water is safe to drink and food hygiene standards are high. However, when exploring remote areas, it's prudent to carry a water purification method, such as tablets or a filter, in case of limited access to clean water sources. Additionally, being mindful of food allergies or dietary restrictions and communicating them clearly when dining out can help prevent adverse reactions.

New Zealand's biosecurity measures are stringent, aiming to protect its unique ecosystems from invasive species and diseases. Travelers should be aware of these regulations and declare any food, plants, or animal products upon entry. Cleaning outdoor gear, such as hiking boots and camping equipment, before arrival can prevent the introduction of foreign contaminants. Adhering to biosecurity guidelines is crucial in preserving New Zealand's natural environment for future generations.

Emergency preparedness is a key component of staying safe while traveling. Familiarizing yourself with local emergency services, including the New Zealand Police, Fire and Emergency New Zealand, and St. John Ambulance, ensures you know who to contact in case of an emergency. The national emergency number is 111, and operators can connect you to the appropriate service. Downloading the Red Cross Hazard App provides real-time alerts and information on natural disasters, such as earthquakes or severe weather events.

Understanding New Zealand's unique natural hazards, such as earthquakes and volcanic activity, is also important. The country is located on the Pacific Ring of Fire, making it prone to seismic activity. While the risk of a significant event is low, knowing how to respond can enhance your safety. In the event of an earthquake, the "Drop, Cover, and Hold" method is recommended, and it's useful to identify safe places in your accommodation or surroundings. Volcanic areas, such as Tongariro National Park, may have specific safety instructions that should be followed closely.

Finally, cultivating a mindset of respect and responsibility towards the environment and local communities enhances both safety and the overall travel experience. Practicing Leave No Trace principles, such as packing out all waste and respecting wildlife, contributes to the preservation of New Zealand's pristine landscapes. Engaging with local communities respectfully and supporting sustainable tourism initiatives fosters positive interactions and enriches your understanding of New Zealand's culture and heritage.

By being informed, prepared, and respectful, travelers can enjoy the myriad experiences New Zealand has to offer while ensuring their health and safety. Each step taken to prioritize well-being not only enhances personal safety but also contributes to the preservation and appreciation of the remarkable environment and communities encountered along the way.

CHAPTER 8: BEYOND THE BEATEN PATH

1. Stewart Island's Unspoiled Wilderness

Stewart Island, or Rakiura as known in Māori, is a pristine jewel at the southern tip of New Zealand, offering a breathtaking glimpse into an unspoiled wilderness where nature reigns supreme. Covering an area of roughly 1,746 square kilometers, the island is predominantly a national park, with over 80% of its land designated as Rakiura National Park since 2002. This dedication to conservation has preserved the island's unique ecosystems, making it a haven for nature lovers and adventure seekers alike.

The journey to Stewart Island begins with a ferry ride across the often tumultuous Foveaux Strait, a 30-kilometer stretch of water that separates the island from the South Island's southern coast. As the ferry approaches Oban, the island's only settlement, visitors are greeted by the sight of lush, verdant hills and a coastline that seems untouched by time. Oban, with its quaint charm and population of just a few hundred residents, serves as the gateway to the island's myriad adventures.

Stewart Island is a paradise for hikers, boasting an extensive network of trails that wind through its diverse landscapes. The Rakiura Track, one of New Zealand's Great Walks, offers a 32-kilometer journey through coastal and forested terrain, taking approximately three days to complete. This track provides an opportunity to immerse oneself in the island's natural beauty, with highlights including expansive sea views, pristine beaches, and dense podocarp forests. For those seeking a more challenging adventure, the North West Circuit offers a 125-kilometer trek that circumnavigates the island, requiring 10 to 12 days to complete. This demanding route traverses remote and rugged terrain, rewarding intrepid hikers with unparalleled solitude and encounters with diverse wildlife.

Stewart Island is renowned for its rich birdlife, with many species found nowhere else in the world. The island's isolation has allowed native birds to thrive, free from the pressures of habitat loss and introduced predators. Birdwatchers will revel in the chance to spot the elusive kiwi, New Zealand's iconic flightless bird, in its natural habitat. Stewart Island is one of the few places where these nocturnal creatures can be seen foraging along beaches and forest floors during the day. Other avian residents include the Stewart Island robin, kaka, and the endangered yellow-eyed penguin, which can be observed nesting along the island's rugged coastline.

The island's waters are equally rich in marine life, offering opportunities for fishing, kayaking, and diving. Anglers can cast a line in pursuit of blue cod, a local delicacy, while kayakers can explore sheltered bays and hidden coves. The crystal-clear waters around Stewart Island provide excellent conditions for diving, with underwater kelp forests and reefs teeming with marine species. The island's marine reserves, such as Ulva Island and Paterson Inlet, are protected areas that allow for the observation of diverse ecosystems, both above and below the waterline.

Ulva Island, a predator-free sanctuary located within Paterson Inlet, is a must-visit for those seeking a deeper connection with Stewart Island's natural world. Accessible by a short boat ride from Oban, Ulva Island is home to a variety of native birds and plants, offering a glimpse into what New Zealand's forests were like before human settlement. The island's well-maintained walking tracks provide a leisurely exploration of its tranquil environment, with the chance to encounter rare species such as the saddleback and the South Island robin.

The island's human history is equally captivating, with a rich tapestry of Māori and European influences. The name Rakiura, meaning "The Land of Glowing Skies," reflects the Māori connection to the island and its natural phenomena, such as the southern lights, or aurora australis, which can occasionally be seen illuminating the night sky. European settlers arrived in the early 19th century, drawn by the island's abundant natural resources, including seals, whales, and timber. Remnants of this history can be found in the form of abandoned whaling stations and sawmills, offering a glimpse into the island's past.

For those seeking a deeper understanding of Stewart Island's cultural heritage, the Rakiura Museum in Oban provides a fascinating insight into the island's history. The museum's exhibits showcase artifacts from both Māori and European settlers, as well as displays on the island's unique flora and fauna. Engaging with local residents, who are often more than willing to share stories and knowledge, can further enrich one's appreciation of the island's heritage and way of life.

Despite its remote location, Stewart Island is not without its comforts. Oban offers a selection of accommodations, from cozy bed-and-breakfasts to self-contained cottages, catering to a range of preferences and budgets. The island's dining options reflect its natural bounty, with fresh seafood and locally sourced ingredients featuring prominently on menus. The local pub, a favorite gathering spot for residents and visitors alike, offers a welcoming atmosphere and the chance to sample a beer brewed with rainwater collected on the island.

Travelers to Stewart Island should come prepared for changeable weather, as the island's maritime climate can bring rapid shifts in conditions. Packing layers, waterproof clothing, and sturdy footwear is advisable, along with essentials such as insect repellent and sunscreen. While the island's remoteness enhances its allure, it also necessitates careful planning, particularly for those undertaking extended hikes or venturing into more isolated areas.

Stewart Island's unspoiled wilderness offers a rare opportunity to disconnect from the modern world and reconnect with nature in its purest form. The island's diverse landscapes, abundant wildlife, and rich cultural heritage create an experience that lingers in the hearts and minds of those fortunate enough to visit. As you explore this remarkable island, you become part of a timeless tapestry, woven from the land, sea, and sky, where each moment is a testament to the enduring beauty and resilience of the natural world.

2. The Chatham Islands Experience

Nestled in the vast expanse of the Pacific Ocean, the Chatham Islands are a remote and captivating destination offering an experience like no other. Located approximately 800 kilometers east of New Zealand's South Island, this archipelago consists of about ten islands, with Chatham and Pitt Islands being the largest and most inhabited. The isolation of the Chathams has preserved a unique blend of Māori, Moriori, and European influences, creating a rich tapestry of history, culture, and natural wonder.

Arriving at the Chatham Islands is an adventure in itself, as travelers typically fly from Christchurch, Wellington, or Auckland, with flights operated by Air Chathams. As the plane descends, the islands emerge as emerald jewels, surrounded by the deep blue of the ocean. The main settlement, Waitangi, serves as the entry point and offers a glimpse into the islanders' way of life, where community, resilience, and resourcefulness are paramount.

The Chatham Islands boast a diverse and rugged landscape, characterized by dramatic coastlines, rolling hills, and expansive wetlands. This varied environment supports a wealth of unique flora and fauna, much of which cannot be found anywhere else in the world. Birdwatchers will be captivated by the islands' avian residents, including the endemic Chatham Island shag, Chatham Island oystercatcher, and black robin, the latter of which was brought back from the brink of extinction thanks to dedicated conservation efforts.

The islands' marine life is equally impressive, with the surrounding waters teeming with fish and marine mammals. The nutrient-rich currents support abundant populations of blue cod, hapuka, and crayfish, making fishing a popular activity for both locals and visitors. Chartering a boat for a fishing expedition offers the chance to experience the thrill of reeling in a prized catch, while also providing a unique perspective on the islands' striking coastline.

Exploring the islands by foot reveals a treasure trove of natural and cultural wonders. The Chatham Islands are home to numerous archaeological sites, including Moriori tree carvings known as dendroglyphs. These carvings, etched into the bark of kopi trees, offer a fascinating insight into the spiritual and cultural practices of the Moriori, the islands' indigenous people. Guided tours led by knowledgeable locals provide an opportunity to learn about the rich history and traditions of the Moriori, as well as the challenges they faced following the arrival of Māori and European settlers.

The island's beaches are a study in contrasts, ranging from the rugged, windswept shores of Ocean Mail Beach to the serene sands of Waitangi Bay. Each beach offers its own unique charm and opportunities for exploration, whether it's beachcombing for shells and fossils or simply soaking in the tranquility of the surroundings. The basalt columns of the Remarkable Rocks, a natural wonder shaped by volcanic activity, are a must-see for geology enthusiasts and provide a striking backdrop for photography.

The Chatham Islands' weather is famously changeable, with conditions often shifting rapidly. Visitors should be prepared for a range of weather scenarios, packing clothing suitable for both warm and cold, wet and dry conditions. The islands' maritime climate ensures that temperatures remain relatively mild throughout the year, but it's always wise to have a waterproof jacket and sturdy shoes on hand for exploring the outdoors.

Cultural experiences are an integral part of the Chatham Islands adventure, with the local community warmly welcoming visitors to share in their way of life. The islands' cuisine is a highlight, featuring an abundance of fresh seafood and locally sourced ingredients. Dining with islanders offers a chance to savor traditional dishes such as pāua patties, crayfish, and muttonbird, while engaging in lively conversation and storytelling.

The annual Chatham Islands Festival, held in January, is a vibrant celebration of the islands' culture and community spirit. The festival showcases local music, dance, arts, and crafts, providing visitors with an opportunity to immerse themselves in the islands' unique atmosphere. Participating in the festival's events and activities fosters connections with islanders and deepens one's appreciation for the resilience and creativity that define the Chatham Islands way of life.

Accommodations on the islands are comfortable and varied, ranging from cozy bed-and-breakfasts to self-contained cottages and lodges. Many of these establishments are family-owned and operated, offering personalized service and insights into island living. Staying in locally owned accommodations not only supports the community but also provides a more authentic and enriching experience.

For those seeking adventure, the Chatham Islands offer a range of outdoor pursuits, from hiking and birdwatching to fishing and diving. The islands' remote location ensures that natural attractions remain largely untouched, allowing visitors to experience the raw beauty of the landscape without the crowds often found in more accessible destinations. Whether trekking through native bush, kayaking along the coastline, or simply enjoying the solitude of a deserted beach, the Chatham Islands provide a sense of escape and connection with nature.

In terms of practical considerations, travelers should be aware that the islands' remote location means that some services and amenities may be limited. It's advisable to bring essential supplies and medications, as well as cash, as not all businesses accept credit cards. Planning ahead and managing expectations ensures a smoother and more enjoyable visit.

The Chatham Islands experience is one of discovery and reflection, where the pace of life slows, and the focus shifts to the natural world and the stories of those who call the islands home. The islands' unique blend of history, culture, and wilderness offers a rare opportunity to step back in time and appreciate the resilience and adaptability of both people and nature. Visitors leave with a profound sense of connection to this remarkable place, carrying with them memories of a land where the past and present coexist in harmony, and where the unspoiled beauty of the environment serves as a reminder of the importance of preserving our planet's fragile ecosystems for future generations.

3. Off-the-Grid Adventures in the Southern Alps

The Southern Alps, a majestic mountain range stretching over 500 kilometers along New Zealand's South Island, offer an unparalleled playground for those seeking off-the-grid adventures. This rugged landscape, characterized by its snow-capped peaks, glacial valleys, and pristine lakes, presents a unique opportunity for intrepid explorers to immerse themselves in the wild beauty of one of the world's most captivating regions. Here, the call of adventure echoes through the valleys, inviting travelers to step away from the comforts of modern life and embrace the challenges and rewards of off-the-grid exploration.

Embarking on an adventure in the Southern Alps requires careful planning and preparation, as the region's remote and often inaccessible terrain can be unforgiving. Ensuring you have the right gear is essential. A high-quality, weather-resistant tent, sleeping bag, and thermal clothing are necessary to withstand the alpine conditions. Additionally, a reliable GPS device, map, and compass will be invaluable in navigating the often-unmarked trails and ensuring you remain on course. It's also vital to pack enough food and water purification tablets, as resupply points are few and far between in these remote areas.

Fiordland National Park, a UNESCO World Heritage site, is a prime location for those seeking solitude and the chance to reconnect with nature. The park's vast wilderness is home to a network of lesser-known trails that lead to hidden gems, such as the stunning Lake Marian, nestled high in the mountains and accessible via a challenging, yet rewarding, trek through lush beech forest. Here, the tranquility of the alpine lake, framed by towering peaks, offers a serene escape from the hustle and bustle of everyday life.

For a more strenuous adventure, consider tackling the Dusky Track, a demanding 84-kilometer route that traverses some of Fiordland's most remote and untouched landscapes. This challenging trek typically takes 8 to 10 days to complete and requires a high level of fitness and experience. The track leads adventurers through dense rainforests, across roaring rivers, and over high mountain passes, rewarding them with breathtaking vistas and the chance to encounter unique wildlife, such as the elusive Fiordland crested penguin and the inquisitive kea.

Mount Aspiring National Park, another jewel of the Southern Alps, offers a myriad of off-the-grid adventures for those willing to venture beyond the well-trodden paths. The park's namesake peak,

Mount Aspiring, known as Tititea in Māori, is a popular destination for mountaineers seeking to conquer its summit. Climbing Mount Aspiring is no small feat and requires technical skills, a guide, and proper equipment. However, those who reach the top are rewarded with panoramic views of the Southern Alps and the satisfaction of having conquered one of New Zealand's most iconic mountains.

For those less inclined to climb, the park also offers a variety of challenging hikes that showcase its diverse landscapes. The Rabbit Pass Route, a demanding trek that crosses high alpine terrain, offers intrepid hikers the chance to experience the raw beauty of the Southern Alps away from the crowds. The route requires navigation skills and careful planning, as weather conditions can change rapidly in the mountains, adding an extra layer of challenge to this off-the-grid adventure.

The Southern Alps are not only a haven for hikers and climbers but also offer thrilling opportunities for backcountry skiing and snowboarding. The region's vast expanses of untouched powder and remote slopes provide an exhilarating playground for those seeking the thrill of carving fresh tracks on pristine snow. Guided tours and heli-skiing experiences offer access to some of the most remote and breathtaking terrain in the Alps, ensuring an unforgettable adventure for snow sports enthusiasts.

Kayaking and packrafting are additional ways to explore the hidden corners of the Southern Alps. The region's rivers, fed by glacial meltwater, carve their way through deep valleys and provide the perfect setting for an off-the-grid paddling adventure. The Hollyford River, with its emerald waters and lush surroundings, offers a picturesque route for kayakers and packrafters, while the more challenging Waiau River provides a thrilling ride through remote and rugged landscapes.

Wild camping in the Southern Alps is an experience that allows adventurers to fully immerse themselves in the natural world. Pitching a tent under a canopy of stars, with the sound of a distant waterfall as a lullaby, offers a sense of freedom and connection with the environment that is hard to replicate elsewhere. It's important to adhere to Leave No Trace principles, ensuring that the pristine beauty of the Alps remains unspoiled for future generations to enjoy.

Safety and environmental stewardship should always be at the forefront of any off-the-grid adventure. The Southern Alps' remote location means that help can be far away, so it's crucial to inform someone of your plans and expected return date. Carrying a personal locator beacon can provide an added layer of security in case of an emergency. Respecting the environment by minimizing impact and following local guidelines ensures the preservation of the region's unique ecosystems.

The allure of the Southern Alps lies in their ability to inspire awe and wonder, offering a reminder of the raw power and beauty of nature. For those willing to venture off the beaten path, the Alps provide a canvas for exploration, adventure, and discovery. Whether conquering a mountain peak, traversing a remote valley, or simply sitting in silence by a crystal-clear lake, the experiences gained in this remarkable region are sure to leave a lasting impression.

In the heart of the Southern Alps, time seems to stand still, and the distractions of the modern world fade away. Here, amidst the towering peaks and untouched wilderness, adventurers find not only the thrill of exploration but also a profound sense of peace and connection with the natural world. As the sun sets behind the mountains, casting a golden glow over the landscape, one can't help but feel a deep appreciation for the simple beauty and enduring power of this extraordinary place.

4. Discovering Hidden Beaches

Nestled along New Zealand's diverse coastline are hidden beaches, each with its own allure and secrets waiting to be unveiled. These secluded gems offer an escape from the bustling tourist spots, inviting those with a spirit of adventure to discover their pristine beauty and tranquil surroundings. With a coastline stretching over 15,000 kilometers, New Zealand is a haven for beach lovers seeking solitude and connection with nature.

The journey to uncover these hidden beaches often begins with a bit of research. Local knowledge, guidebooks, and online forums can provide valuable hints about less-frequented spots. Once armed with this information, the adventure truly begins. Many of these beaches are accessible only by foot, requiring a trek through native bush or along rugged cliffs, adding a sense of anticipation as you draw closer to the shore.

One such hidden gem is New Chums Beach, located on the Coromandel Peninsula. This beach, consistently ranked among the world's finest, remains untouched by development and can only be reached by a 30-minute walk from Whangapoua Beach. The trek takes you through a grove of pohutukawa trees and across a tidal stream, culminating in the breathtaking sight of golden sands and azure waters. The seclusion of New Chums Beach offers a perfect setting for sunbathing, swimming, or simply unwinding in the serenity of nature.

Venturing further south, the Taranaki region boasts the striking Back Beach. Here, volcanic black sands meet the roaring Tasman Sea, creating a dramatic and rugged landscape. Accessible via a short walk from the city of New Plymouth, Back Beach is a favorite among locals for its surf and stunning views of the Sugar Loaf Islands. The beach's ever-changing tides and windswept dunes provide a dynamic environment, perfect for those seeking a more active beach experience.

On the South Island, the Catlins Coast is home to Purakaunui Bay, a secluded cove surrounded by towering cliffs and native bush. The journey to Purakaunui Bay involves navigating gravel roads and forested trails, adding to the sense of discovery. As you emerge onto the beach, the sight of its sweeping sands and crystal-clear waters is a reward in itself. This hidden treasure is ideal for a peaceful picnic, exploration of rock pools, or simply soaking in the breathtaking coastal scenery.

The remote beaches of Abel Tasman National Park offer another enchanting escape. While the park is well-known, some of its beaches remain less trodden, thanks to their remote locations accessible only by kayak or on foot. Anchorage Bay, for example, can be reached via a scenic coastal track or a leisurely paddle through turquoise waters. The beach's golden sands and lush backdrop provide a tranquil retreat, where visitors can enjoy activities such as swimming, snorkeling, or simply basking in the sun.

Travelers seeking an even more isolated experience may venture to Stewart Island, where the beaches offer unparalleled solitude and natural beauty. Mason Bay, accessible through a multi-day hike or a boat trip, is one of the island's most remote beaches. Here, miles of untouched sand stretch against a backdrop of windswept dunes and dense forest. The isolation of Mason Bay attracts those with a passion for birdwatching, as the beach is a favored habitat for the iconic kiwi and other native bird species.

When exploring these hidden beaches, preparation is key. The remote locations often mean limited access to amenities, so it's essential to pack accordingly. Water, snacks, sun protection, and appropriate footwear are must-haves for any beach expedition. Additionally, a sense of adventure and respect for the environment will ensure a rewarding experience.

Understanding the tides and weather conditions is also crucial when visiting these secluded spots. New Zealand's weather can be unpredictable, and coastal conditions can change rapidly. Checking the forecast and tide schedules before setting out can help avoid any unexpected challenges and ensure a safe and enjoyable visit.

Interacting with the local community can enhance the experience of discovering hidden beaches. Locals often have insider knowledge about the best times to visit, potential hazards, and unique features of each beach. Engaging in conversation and showing appreciation for their insights can lead to memorable encounters and a deeper connection to the area.

Caring for the environment is paramount when visiting these pristine locations. Practicing Leave No Trace principles, such as packing out all trash and respecting wildlife, helps preserve the natural beauty of these beaches for future generations. Being mindful of the impact of human activity ensures that these hidden treasures remain unspoiled and accessible for years to come.

Each hidden beach in New Zealand offers a unique experience, shaped by its distinct landscape and the journey required to reach it. Whether it's the thrill of discovery, the allure of solitude, or the chance to connect with nature, these secluded shores provide a sense of fulfillment and wonder. As you explore these hidden gems, you'll find that the true reward lies not only in the destination but in the journey itself. The memories created and the stories gathered along the way become cherished souvenirs of a land where the sea meets the sand in perfect harmony.

5. Unique Experiences in Remote Villages

Amidst the breathtaking landscapes of New Zealand, remote villages offer unique experiences that allow travelers to immerse themselves in the local culture and traditions. These hidden gems, often overlooked by mainstream tourism, provide a window into the authentic way of life that has remained largely unchanged for generations. The journey to these villages is not just about reaching a destination; it's about embracing the stories, customs, and rhythms of the people who inhabit these secluded corners of the world.

Nestled in the heart of the North Island, the village of Whangamomona stands as a testament to resilience and community spirit. Known as the "Republic of Whangamomona," this village declared itself an independent republic in 1989 as a playful protest against regional council boundaries. Every two years, the village hosts Republic Day, a lively festival where visitors can experience a blend of local humor, hospitality, and tradition. The festivities feature sheep races, gumboot throwing, and a chance to obtain an official Whangamomona passport, making for an unforgettable experience that leaves a lasting impression.

Traveling to the South Island, the village of Okains Bay on Banks Peninsula offers a deep dive into Māori heritage and culture. Home to the Okains Bay Māori and Colonial Museum, this village preserves a rich collection of artifacts that tell the story of the Ngāi Tahu people and the early European settlers. Visitors can explore traditional Māori buildings, including a wharenui (meeting house), and gain insights into the customs and practices that have shaped the region's history. Engaging with local Māori guides provides an opportunity to learn about the significance of these traditions and their enduring importance in contemporary New Zealand.

In the remote expanses of the South Island's West Coast, the village of Karamea beckons adventurers with its untamed beauty and warm community spirit. This village serves as the gateway to the Kahurangi National Park and the famous Heaphy Track, attracting hikers and nature enthusiasts eager to explore the region's diverse landscapes. Beyond its natural wonders, Karamea is known for its vibrant arts scene, with local artisans showcasing their work in galleries and studios. Visitors can meet the artists, learn about their creative processes, and even participate in workshops to create their own unique pieces.

Heading north to the East Cape, the village of Te Araroa offers a glimpse into a slower pace of life, where the sunrise first touches the shores of New Zealand. This village is home to the ancient pōhutukawa tree known as Te Waha-o-Rerekohu, believed to be over 600 years old. The local iwi (tribe) share stories of the tree's significance and its connection to the land and people. With its unspoiled beaches and rich cultural heritage, Te Araroa invites visitors to unwind and appreciate the simple joys of life, from fishing and gathering shellfish to listening to tales passed down through generations.

Further inland, the village of Naseby in Central Otago offers a unique blend of history and recreation. Known as the curling capital of New Zealand, Naseby provides visitors with the chance to try their hand at this traditional ice sport. The Maniototo Curling International Rink offers lessons and games year-round, allowing visitors to experience the camaraderie and skill involved in curling. The village's rich gold-mining history is also evident in its heritage buildings and museums, where stories of fortune seekers and pioneers come to life.

The village of Stewart Island, although technically an island and not a village, exudes a close-knit community atmosphere that makes it feel like one. As New Zealand's third-largest island, it offers a wealth of natural attractions, from the pristine beaches of Rakiura National Park to the abundant birdlife that calls the island home. Visitors can join guided tours led by locals who share their knowledge of the island's flora and fauna, as well as the challenges and rewards of living in such a remote location. The island's limited infrastructure and reliance on community resources foster a sense of self-sufficiency and cooperation that is both inspiring and humbling.

When visiting these remote villages, it's important to approach with respect and an open mind. Each village has its own customs and traditions, and taking the time to learn about and honor these practices enhances the experience for both visitors and residents. Engaging with locals through conversation and participation in community events fosters mutual understanding and creates lasting connections.

Practical considerations are essential when planning a visit to these remote villages. Access can be limited, with some locations requiring travel on gravel roads or by boat. Packing essentials such as food, water, and appropriate clothing ensures a comfortable journey. Additionally, supporting local businesses and services not only enriches the travel experience but also contributes to the sustainability and vitality of these communities.

Unique experiences in remote villages offer more than just a getaway; they provide a chance to step into a world where time moves at a different pace, where stories are shared around a communal table, and where the bonds between people and place are woven tightly together. These villages may exist far from the beaten path, but their impact on the heart and mind is profound, leaving visitors with a deeper appreciation for the diverse tapestry of life that exists beyond the urban landscape. Embracing the unknown, listening to the stories of those who call these villages home, and sharing in their daily lives is a journey of discovery that enriches the soul and broadens horizons.

CONCLUSION AND FAREWELL

Reflecting on the journey through these diverse and captivating landscapes, the tapestry of experiences woven together forms a vibrant picture of discovery, adventure, and cultural immersion. Each chapter has unraveled unique stories, painting a vivid portrait of the places visited and the people met along the way. From the rugged challenges of the Southern Alps to the tranquil embrace of hidden beaches, from the intriguing histories of remote villages to the exhilarating off-the-grid adventures, the essence of exploration is captured in the richness of these encounters.

In the heart of this journey lies a profound appreciation for the natural world and the communities that thrive within it. The landscapes we've traversed are not just backdrops but living entities, each with its own rhythm, challenges, and rewards. Engaging with these environments has taught us the value of resilience and adaptability, as well as the importance of preserving the delicate balance that sustains them.

The people encountered throughout these travels have shared their lives, customs, and stories, enriching our understanding of the world. Their hospitality and openness have provided insights into the traditions and values that define their communities. It's in these interactions that the true spirit of travel is found—bridging cultures, fostering mutual respect, and creating connections that transcend geographical boundaries.

As we bid farewell to this exploration, it's essential to carry forward the lessons learned and the memories made. Each experience adds a layer to our personal narrative, shaping our perspectives and inspiring future journeys. The adventures chronicled here serve as a reminder of the beauty and diversity that await those who dare to step off the beaten path.

The journey doesn't end here, for the world is vast and filled with endless possibilities. The call to explore, to seek out the unknown, and to embrace the unfamiliar will continue to resonate. As travelers, we are part of a global community bound by a shared curiosity and a desire to understand the world and our place within it.

In the end, the essence of travel is not just about the destinations reached but the transformative power of the journey itself. It's about the stories we gather, the friendships we forge, and the insights we gain. As we close this chapter, may the memories of these adventures inspire new dreams, ignite the spark of wanderlust, and remind us of the endless wonders that lie just beyond the horizon.

To all who have joined in this journey, may your paths be filled with discovery and your hearts with the joy of exploration. The world awaits, ready to reveal its secrets to those who venture forth with open eyes and an open heart. Until we meet again on another road, in another place, the adventure continues.

BONUS 1: ESSENTIAL PHRASES FOR YOUR DAILY TRAVEL NEEDS IN NEW ZEALAND

BONUS 2: PRINTABLE TRAVEL JOURNAL

BONUS 3: 10 TIPS "THAT CAN SAVE THE DAY" ON YOUR TRIP IN NEW ZEALAND

Made in United States
Troutdale, OR
12/28/2024

27359438R00086